Sharing the Gift of

Encouragement

BY

Charles F. Stanley

Thomas Nelson
Since 1798

Sharing the Gift of Encouragement

Charles F. Stanley

Copyright © 1998, 2008 by Charles F. Stanley

Published in Nashville, Tennessee, by Thomas Nelson, Inc.

GↃB

Editing, layout, and design by Gregory C. Benoit Publishing, Old Mystic, CT

ISBN 1-4185-2812-9

Printed in the United States of America

HB 02.12.2024

Contents

Sharing the Gift of Encouragement

This is not an inspirational book; it is a study manual linked to the Bible. While reading, you will refer to your Bible again and again, and I hope that you will freely mark phrases and words that have special meaning to you, or write in the margins what God is speaking to you in your spirit.

Many good inspirational and devotional books are on the market today. I certainly recommend that you read daily from those authors who love God's Word and help apply it to daily living in an encouraging, inspirational way. The Bible, however, will always remain the most encouraging book ever written. It is the source from which we draw our hope and faith. It is the reference to which we must return again and again to make certain that the words we speak to others are not just idle words that flow from our human desire, but are words that are in line with *God's* hopes and desires.

In this study we will be focusing on several key aspects of encouragement. As you read and study the Scriptures as a whole, you will encounter "encouragement in action" time and time again. The *whole* of God's message on encouragement cannot be contained in a Bible study book or course. It is far too great for that. It is to be found only in a full understanding of *all* of God's Word. I trust that you are reading and studying the Bible on a daily basis.

This book can be used by you alone or by several people in a small-group study. At various times, you will be asked to relate to the material in one of these four ways:

1. *What new insights have you gained?* Make notes about the insights

that you have. You may want to record them in your Bible or in a separate journal. As you reflect back over your insights, you are likely to see how God has moved in your life.

2. *Have you ever had a similar experience?* Each of us approaches the Bible from a unique background—our own particular set of relationships and experiences. Our experiences do not make the Bible true—the Word of God is truth regardless of our opinion about it. It is important, however, to share our experiences in order to see how God's truth can be applied to human lives.

3. *How do you feel about the material presented?* Emotional responses do not give validity to the Scriptures, nor should we trust our emotions as a gauge for our faith. In small-group Bible study, however, it is good for participants to express their emotions. The Holy Spirit often communicates with us through this unspoken language.

4. *In what way do you feel challenged to respond or to act?* God's Word may cause you to feel inspired or challenged to change something in your life. Take the challenge seriously and find ways of acting upon it. If God reveals to you a particular need that He wants *you* to address, take that as "marching orders" from God. God is expecting you to *do* something with the challenge that He has just given you.

Start and conclude your Bible study sessions in prayer. Ask God to give you spiritual eyes to see and spiritual ears to hear. As you conclude your study, ask the Lord to seal what you have learned so that you will never forget it. Ask Him to help you grow into the fullness of the stature of Christ Jesus.

Again, I caution you to keep the Bible at the center of your study. A genuine Bible study stays focused on God's Word and promotes a growing faith and a closer walk with the Holy Spirit in *each* person who participates.

LESSON 1

Our Need for Encouragement

ᐧᐦ In This Lesson ᐦᐧ

LEARNING: WHAT'S SO IMPORTANT ABOUT ENCOURAGEMENT?

GROWING: HOW CAN I FIND ENCOURAGEMENT MYSELF?

Every person I know could use more encouragement—and not just a little more encouragement, but a *lot* more encouragement. For the most part, our world is experiencing a drought of encouraging words, uplifting examples, genuine heroes, "good news" stories, and genuine expressions of appreciation. We hear far more negative words of criticism, blame, and ridicule on a daily basis than we hear positive words of praise, recognition, and thankfulness.

Why is it that each of us has a deep need for encouragement, and yet so little encouragement is to be found? I believe the foremost reason is that so few people feel encouraged in their own spirits. It is very difficult to share with others something that you do not feel yourself. Encouragement is rooted in the following:

ᐧᐦ **God's love:** understanding and believing that God loves you and has forgiven you—completely

ᐧᐦ **Dignity:** feeling as if one has a "position" in Christ

❧ *Respect*: feeling as if one has a right to be treated as one of God's beloved children

Above all, encouragement is grounded in unconditional love. A person needs to feel truly loved for who he is as a unique and valued creation of God; otherwise, he is not going to *feel* encouraged. Such love must be received regardless of the person's actions, traits, or accomplishments. It must not be love that is granted for manipulative purposes. It must be love that is both *perceived* and actively *received* without any strings or conditions attached.

The prerequisite to encouraging others is to feel encouraged yourself.

The Message of Encouragement

Encouragement has a very basic message: *Your past and present do not need to continue into your future.* What is a reality today does not need to be what will be the reality of tomorrow. If you are feeling unloved, you can feel love. If you are weighed down under a load of guilt, you can receive forgiveness. If you are wallowing in a cloud of confusion, you can experience God's wisdom and guidance. If your life is in turmoil, you can have peace in your heart. If you are alone and rejected, you can be accepted and surrounded by genuine Christian friends.

Encouragement is speaking a word of hope. It is expressing to another person the sure certainty that God created you with a great potential for good and that God desires to help you fulfill your potential. Your future can be better than your past or present. You can grow and develop and be ever more transformed into the likeness of Jesus Christ. You can experience greater fulfillment and wholeness than you are presently. You can have an even more abundant life than the one that you presently have.

Those who are discouraged tend to feel that they are locked into their present position—emotionally, spiritually, physically, materially. Encouragement is saying to that imprisoned person, "God has the keys to your prison! He can make a way out of your present circumstances and situation where you do not see a way. He can sovereignly change hearts and remove roadblocks."

The message of encouragement is that we can survive the assaults of the devil against our lives, we can endure the persecution that comes our way, we can be victorious over the circumstances that assail us, and in the midst of any kind of trial, trouble, or tribulation, we can know God's peace and joy. The message of encouragement is a triple-packed message of God's goodness, the hope that we have in Christ Jesus, and the omnipotent power of the Holy Spirit at work in us, through us, and on our behalf!

The Foundation for Encouragement

On what basis is encouragement given? On the sure foundation that God loves His children and desires their highest good. If you do not believe that God is a loving God, or if you do not believe that God is continually at work bringing all things to good for those who are His children, then you probably are not encouraged in your own spirit—and you cannot encourage others. On the other hand, if you know that God is a loving, merciful, forgiving God—always desiring our best and working to give us His perfect good—then encouragement is within your grasp and you can share it.

Before you can share encouragement with others, you must come to a firm resolve within yourself regarding what you believe about four things:

1. God's nature

2. Jesus Christ and His work on the cross

3. the relationship that God desires with His children

4. the work of the Holy Spirit in the world today

Encouragement flows from what you believe. It is *always* an expression of your faith in God. Conversely, discouraging words are always an expression of a *lack of faith* in God. Guard your words. But above all, build up your faith. The heart that is strong in faith is a heart that will naturally overflow in encouragement.

The Call to Encouragement

As Christians, we are called by God to encourage others. We read in Scripture that we are to "love the brotherhood" with a fervent and pure spirit (1 Peter 1:22, 2:17). We are to build up one another in faith (Jude 20). We are to remind one another of the goodness and love of God (1 John 1:1–4).

The expression of encouragement is always to be active. We are not merely to be an encouragement to others through our example of a virtuous life. We are to *share* encouragement by voicing words of encouragement and engaging in specific deeds. Encouragement is not merely something that we *are*, it is something that we *do*.

Throughout the Gospels and the New Testament letters we find strong words of encouragement. Jesus is our supreme role model of encouragement. Every one of His miracle works was an act of encouragement. He described His own ministry in this way in Luke 4:18–19:

The Spirit of the LORD is upon Me,
Because He has anointed Me to preach the gospel to the poor.
He has sent Me to heal the brokenhearted,
To preach deliverance to the captives
And recovery of sight to the blind,
To set at liberty those who are oppressed,
To preach the acceptable year of the LORD.

What an encouraging world we would live in if all Christians followed Christ's example and preached good news to the poor, healed the brokenhearted, proclaimed freedom to the captives and recovery of sight to the blind, set free the oppressed, and proclaimed the gospel of Jesus Christ, our Lord! Jesus plainly said that He came *not* to condemn the world, but that "the world through Him might be saved" (John 3:17). The message of salvation is the most encouraging message that we can ever share.

The apostle John wrote (1 John 2:12–14):

I write to you, little children,
  Because your sins are
    forgiven you for His name's sake.
I write to you, fathers,
  Because you have known
    Him who is from the beginning.
I write to you, young men,
  Because you have overcome
    the wicked one.
I write to you, little children,
  Because you have known
    the Father.
I have written to you, fathers,
  Because you have known

Him who is from the beginning.
I have written to you, young men,
Because you are strong, and
the word of God abides in you,
And you have overcome the wicked one.

What wonderful words of encouragement! John always referred to himself as the "beloved disciple," and he was a giver of love to others with an intent that they be built up in Christ, and in turn, love one another generously and without fear.

Again and again we see in the New Testament the message of hope, of change, of growth, of victorious living. What we have received in Christ, and what we have been given in His Word, we are called by God to give to others. We are not called to be doomsday prophets, pessimists, down-in-the-mouth naysayers, or condemning critics. We are called to encourage!

Choose to be encouraged today, then choose to share encouragement.

∂. What new insights into encouragement do you hope to gain from this study?

∂. When have you received valuable encouragement from someone?

❧ When have you been very discouraged by someone's words to you?

❧ In general, are you a source of *encouragement* or *discouragement* to others?

❧ Today and Tomorrow ❧

TODAY: THE FOUNDATION OF ENCOURAGEMENT IS BUILT UPON THE LOVE AND ACCEPTANCE OF GOD.

TOMORROW: I WILL SPEND TIME IN GOD'S WORD AND PRAYER THIS WEEK, MEDITATING ON THE LOVE OF GOD.

LESSON 2

You Are God's Beloved

───── ❧ **In This Lesson** ☙ ─────

LEARNING: WHY IS GOD'S LOVE SO IMPORTANT TO ENCOURAGEMENT?

GROWING: HOW DO I *KNOW* THAT GOD LOVES ME?

∞

God loves you. Let the words sink into your spirit. They are three of the most encouraging words that you can ever hear or speak. People in our world today are starving for God's love. Most people receive very little affirmation in their lives and very little love. Adults have readily confessed to me with tears in their eyes, "I never heard my father say that he loves me."

I know how they feel. My father died when I was only nine months old, and so I have no recollection of his telling me that he loved me. My mother married my stepfather—a hard and critical man—when I was nine years old, and I never heard him say that he loved me. Neither did I ever receive anything from him that was presented with affection or personal concern. I know the loneliness in spirit that can develop if a person grows up aching to hear words of approval and love.

For years in my ministry, I did not "feel" the love of God in my heart. I knew that He loved me on the basis of His Word, but I did not have a "feeling" that He loved me. I had been a pastor for many years before I had an experience in which I truly felt the love of God filling my heart.

It was an experience that I wish every person could have. There's nothing as glorious this side of heaven as knowing that God loves you with an infinite, unconditional love and that it is out of His love that He has created you, forgiven you, and received you fully as His beloved child.

The Hallmarks of God's Love

Let me share two great truths about God's love for you:

1. *God loves each one of us unconditionally and absolutely.* God's love is absolute, and it does not change over time or according to your behavior. God's love is not influenced by circumstances, and it cannot be diminished. God can never love you more than He loves you today, and neither can He love you less. He loves you because He created you—and because He *chooses* to love you, now and every moment of your life. Nothing can separate you from God's love (Romans 8:35–39).

2. *God loves us first.* God does not wait for us to come to Him with an expression of love before He extends love to us. On the contrary, God loves us first. John said it simply and eloquently: "We love Him because He first loved us" (1 John 4:19). God is always waiting with open arms, ready to receive those who turn to Him. He longs to embrace us, forgive us, restore us to full fellowship with Him, and to bless us as His children.

> For I am persuaded that neither death nor life, nor angels nor principalities nor powers, nor things present nor things to come, nor height nor depth, nor any other created thing, shall be able to separate us from the love of God which is in Christ Jesus our Lord.
>
> —Romans 8:38-39

∾ How secure do you feel in God's love? What, if anything, makes you wonder sometimes whether God still loves you?

∾ What present circumstances have you worried? What future possibilities? How do these verses encourage you in those fears?

What an encouraging word, that nothing—absolutely nothing—can separate us from God's love for us. His love is always extended to you and to me. It is our responsibility to accept His love and delight in it. Those who do so enjoy an inner freedom and encouragement that they cannot experience by any other means.

∾

Why Some Don't Believe that God Loves Them

There are a number of reasons that people fail to experience the love of God, but in this lesson I want to focus on three of them. Often when we seek to encourage another person who is "down" in spirit, we will find one of these factors at the root of their discouragement. People do not believe that God loves them because:

෬ They have never had a role model of God's love.

෬ They have been taught incorrectly about God.

෬ They have gone through difficulties that they believe a loving God should have spared them.

∞ Lack of Role Models ∞

My lack of understanding about God's love came largely from a lack of role models. I knew that my mother loved me, but she was the only person in my childhood who (as far as I knew) loved me to the point of being there for me if times were tough. It isn't enough to have someone tell you that he loves you. The person must *be there for you* when you need him.

We need to experience love in tangible, physical forms. We need the presence, comfort, and touch of other people. We especially need this when we are experiencing pain, depression, loneliness, crises, and hard times. We need love that has "arms" that will hold us, comfort us, and say, "God loves you, and so do I."

෬ When has someone expressed love to you—not only in words, but in their physical presence? How did you feel?

Jesus knew this human need for an abiding presence of love. He spent much of His last evening before the crucifixion *commanding* His disciples to "love one another" (John 15:17).

One of the central teachings in the early church was that Christians were to be role models of God's love one to another. John wrote, "If God so loved us, we also ought to love one another" (1 John 4:11). If you have never experienced the love of God through other people, then find a fellowship of Christian believers where that love is flowing freely and purely, not just in lip service. Find a church where people are serving one another and ministering to one another with a loving attitude. Choose also to be an agent of God's love. Be a role model for others of God's loving presence.

⤞ Who has been a good role model for God's love in your life?

And we have known and believed the love that God has for us. God is love, and he who abides in love abides in God, and God in him.

—1 John 4:16

⤞ What does it mean to "abide in love"? Are you abiding in God's love this week, or on the outside looking in?

∾ Incorrect Teaching ∾

Many people have grown up from their childhoods with a false under-standing of God. If you are such a person, I invite you today to relearn what is true about God. God is not a harsh judge with a long, white beard, sitting on His throne just waiting to pounce on you for doing wrong. That is a picture that has been painted by some people, but that is not the picture that is presented in the New Testament! The Bible teaches us that God's very nature is love. God's mercy always balances His righteousness (1 John 4:14–16).

The psalmist speaks repeatedly of God's loving kindness. It is on the basis of God's love that we can hope for God's salvation, ongoing provi-sion, and deliverance in times of trouble (Psalm 36:7–8, 10–11). God sent Jesus into the world because of His love. The most famous verse in all the Bible assures us of this: "God so loved the world that He gave His only begotten Son" (John 3:16).

God desires to reveal Himself to you today as a loving Father—one who will protect you, provide for you, forgive you, help you, bless you, en-courage you, and uplift you. His arms are open wide to you. He longs to shower His love and good gifts upon you. He also longs to be loved *by* you. He wants to be in a loving relationship with you so that you share your heart fully with Him and He, in turn, shares Himself fully with you. What encouraging news to our soul, and what encouraging news to share with others!

Beloved, let us love one another, for love is of God; and everyone who loves is born of God and knows God.

—1 John 4:7

🔊 Have you been born again into the family of God? If not, what is preventing you from accepting Christ as your Savior right now?

🔊 If you have been born again into God's family, what does this verse suggest about the influence of love in your life?

∽ All Things for Good ∽

A third reason that people do not believe that God loves them is that they have a false understanding of how God might use difficulties that come into a person's life. They falsely believe God to be the instigator of trouble. They end up blaming God for every tragedy, disappointment, or crisis that comes their way. They ask, "How could God love me and allow this terrible thing to happen to me?"

The Bible teaches very clearly that good and bad times happen to believers and unbelievers alike. No person is immune to life's circumstances, both positive and negative (Matthew 5:45). We live in a fallen world in which both evil and good exist. At no time are we told that God spares Christians from all temptations, trials, or problems. We can be assured, however, that God is *with* us and remains with us when trouble strikes, and that He can use the trial to accomplish a good purpose in our lives. God assures His people that He will never leave them nor forsake them (Deuteronomy 31:6, 8; Joshua 1:5; Hebrews 13:5).

God wants us to be whole—spirit, mind, and body—and His purposes for us are always for our ultimate good. When we experience a time of difficulty, our first question should not be "Why me, God?" but rather, "God, what good are you desiring to work in me and through me?" God's purpose in allowing difficulty into our lives is so that He might either correct us from error or further refine in us those things that are good. We are constantly in a state of being:

    ❧ **Purified**—all impurities of sin being burned away from us

    ❧ **Perfected**—all good things in us being strengthened.

The process of purification is called "chastisement" or "chastening" in the Scriptures. When we are being chastened, God is calling us to turn away from things that are evil or harmful. He does not want us to suffer the terrible consequences of sin.

We are assured that "whom the LORD loves He chastens" (Hebrews 12:6). God's process is not one of *punishment*, which is a response to negative behavior, but of *correction*, which has a teaching component to it. God's intent is that we learn a positive lesson so that we might change our ways, grow spiritually, and receive an even greater blessing from our loving heavenly Father. Just as any loving parent, God corrects us and teaches us *for our good.*

The perfecting process is one of ongoing learning; in times of difficulty, the Lord strengthens those character traits in us that are godly. It is in times of trouble that we learn how to apply God's wisdom, love, and power. In many ways, the traits of self-control, endurance in faith, and true godliness are forged in the fires of suffering (2 Peter 1:5–8). The purpose of God in perfecting us is that we might become more useful servants in God's kingdom—our witness might be brighter, our service more productive and effective. God loves us enough to want us to grow up into the very likeness of Jesus Christ, His beloved Son!

> ...He makes His sun rise on the evil and on the good, and sends rain on the just and on the unjust.
>
> —Matthew 5:45

What does this verse teach you about the blessings of life? About suffering?

According to this verse, what do we do to "earn" God's blessings, or to "deserve" His chastisements?

And we know that all things work together for good to those

who love God, to those who are the called according to His purpose.

—Romans 8:28

⇜ What people are "the called according to God's purpose"? Are you one of those people?

⇜ What suffering have you gone through that has actually brought blessings in the end?

My son, do not despise the chastening of the Lord, nor be discouraged when you are rebuked by Him; for whom the Lord
loves He chastens, and scourges every son whom He receives.

—Hebrews 12:5-6

Why does God, the loving Father, "scourge every son whom
He receives"? How can God be loving and scourging at the same
time?

Why should we not become discouraged when we are rebuked by God? Where can we find encouragement in that situation? What does the rebuking itself prove to us?

Today and Tomorrow

TODAY: GOD LOVES ME COMPLETELY AND UNCONDITIONALLY, AND SUFFER-
ING IS ACTUALLY A PROOF OF THIS.

TOMORROW: I WILL SPEND TIME THIS WEEK PRAISING GOD FOR LOVING ME
ENOUGH TO MAKE ME LIKE CHRIST.

LESSON 3

You Can Receive Forgiveness

─────── ⊷ **In This Lesson** ℘ ───────

LEARNING: WHAT, EXACTLY, DO YOU MEAN BY "FORGIVENESS"?

GROWING: HOW CAN I EVER HOPE TO BE LESS SINFUL?

⊷℘⊶

You can be forgiven! No matter what sin you have committed, you can be cleansed by God. No matter how much guilt and shame you feel, you can be forgiven and have a newness of spirit. God's Word is absolute on these truths. The assurance of God's ever-present and free offer of forgiveness is one of the most encouraging truths that a person can ever share. It is through forgiveness that we genuinely experience a newness of life and are given the gift of eternal life.

The Nature of God's Forgiveness

There are five great truths about God's forgiveness that I want to focus on in this lesson:

1. God's forgiveness is offered to all, but it must be actively received.

2. God's provision for forgiveness is the shed blood of Jesus Christ.

3. When we receive God's forgiveness, we are given a new spiritual nature.

4. When God forgives, God forgets.

5. In our relationships with others, we experience forgiveness *as* we forgive those who have wronged us.

∞ Receiving God's Gift of Forgiveness ∞

God's forgiveness is extended to all, but not everybody receives it. God's forgiveness is offered freely, but it is not given without a conscious, deliberate act of acceptance. There are those who believe that God automatically and universally forgives everybody. That is not the message of the Bible. God's forgiveness must be *received*. This is an act of the human will. Part of God's creation of mankind is that we have the privilege to refuse or to accept God's offer of forgiveness and love—we are not forced to receive it. Neither are we automatically forgiven. We must turn to God and intentionally receive forgiveness.

To receive God's forgiveness, one must first acknowledge within oneself the need for forgiveness and reconciliation to God. When we confess to ourselves and to God that we are in need of forgiveness and turn to Him to receive it, He grants forgiveness freely and unconditionally.

> If we confess our sins, He is faithful and just to forgive us our sins and to cleanse us from all unrighteousness.
>
> —1 John 1:9

∞ Have you deliberately asked God to forgive your sins? If not, what is stopping you?

~ If you know that your sins are forgiven, do you remember frequently to rejoice and give thanks for that gift?

∞ Jesus' Death Makes Forgiveness Possible ∞

God's offer of forgiveness is based upon the sacrificial death of Jesus Christ. Adam and Eve sinned against God through their willful disobedience in the Garden of Eden, and they caused all of mankind to be plunged into sin. Every person is born with a sin nature that separates him spiritually from God.

God provided a bridge over this sin-nature chasm: In the Old Testament, this bridge was in the form of animal sacrifices. The shedding of blood was required for the forgiveness of sin. God required man to recognize in a very tangible form that He is the author of all life and that no true wholeness of life can be experienced apart from Him.

The supreme and definitive sacrifice for sin was made when God offered His own Son, Jesus Christ, on the cross. Jesus died on the cross, shedding His blood as a sin-free "lamb" without any blemish, taking on Himself the sins of the world. His sacrificial death eliminated the need for any further sacrifice. The blood of Jesus purchased salvation from sin once and for all time. Jesus said in John 3:14–15:

> As Moses lifted up the serpent in the wilderness, even so must the Son of Man be lifted up, that whoever believes in Him should not perish but have eternal life.

23

In the Old Testament, a plague of deadly vipers came upon the children of Israel, and God commanded Moses to make a bronze serpent and place it on a pole. Anyone bitten by a viper would survive—if they looked at the bronze serpent with faith in God. Those who did not look with faith in God died (Numbers 21:1–9). Jesus said that He would be lifted up on the cross in the same way, so that all who "looked" on Him with faith would be saved from their sin and receive the gift of eternal life (John 3:16).

Jesus Christ is God's means for receiving His forgiveness. He has made no other provision. Jesus said very plainly that He was the way to salvation (John 14:6).

> Jesus said to him, "I am the way, the truth, and the life. No one comes to the Father except through Me."
>
> —John 14:6

☙ This statement of Jesus was very controversial in His day—and still is today. How does His claim compare with the teachings of the world?

☙ What does it mean to come to the Father "through Jesus"? How is this done?

∞ God Forgives the Old and Gives the New ∞

When we receive God's forgiveness, we are given a completely new nature. Our old spiritual nature—with all of its desire for self and sin—is cleansed from us. Our hearts are made new, and our new spiritual nature has a desire for God and a desire to follow His commandments. This change in our spiritual nature is so complete that the best way to describe it is that we are "born again" in our spirits (John 3:5–8).

When a baby is born, he has no memory of what it was like to be inside his mother's womb. Everything about the baby's life is changed at birth: he breathes air, experiences the weight of gravity, and has a completely new sensation of touch. He cries, takes in nourishment through his mouth, grows in self-awareness and awareness of others, sees light, and experiences many other changes. The same is true for the person who is born anew spiritually. Everything about one's spiritual perception and experience is changed.

> Therefore, if anyone is in Christ, he is a new creation; old things have passed away; behold, all things have become new.
>
> —2 Corinthians 5:17

∞ What are the "old things" that passed away when you were saved? What things have "become new"?

∞ How can you be encouraged by the loss of those "old things" and the "renewal" of good things?

⋖ God Forgives and Forgets ⋗

When God forgives, God forgets. Forgiveness from God results in a complete "fresh start" from God's perspective. Nothing of the old is remembered or counted against a person. No matter how many times a person errs or sins against God after he is saved, he can be forgiven and experience a new beginning. Any time we turn to God with a sincere heart and admit our failures, shortcomings, and willful rebellion, God hears our prayer and responds with forgiveness. Once we are forgiven, we stand before God totally cleansed. God never holds our past sin against us.

> As far as the east is from the west, So far has He removed our transgressions from us.

> —Psalm 103:12

⋙ Imagine circling the earth, heading from north to south. Eventually, you will begin to travel back up from south to north. Why, then, does David write "as far as the east is from the west"?

⋙ What does this suggest about God's forgiveness?

∞ Forgiven As We Forgive ∞

Some people live with guilt, shame, and other lingering negative feelings of anger and bitterness—not because they have failed to believe in Jesus Christ or failed to receive God's forgiveness, but because they have not forgiven other people. God's Word is very clear on this: "Forgive, and you will be forgiven" (Luke 6:37). When we forgive others, releasing them from our hearts, we experience great freedom of spirit.

Heaviness of heart is not necessarily a product of sin against God. It can be the result of holding a grudge, continuing to bear resentment, or harboring bitterness against others. Hate and a spirit of vengeance can weigh down the soul. Choose to be free! Forgive those who have done evil against you. Entrust them to God.

> And whenever you stand praying, if you have anything against anyone, forgive him, that your Father in heaven may also forgive you your trespasses. But if you do not forgive, neither will your Father in heaven forgive your trespasses.
>
> —Mark 11:25-26

∞ What grudges or resentments are you clinging to?

∞ Take time to pray, right now, telling God that you choose to forgive the people listed above.

What encouraging news that God makes a way for every person to experience freedom from guilt and shame. God freely offers forgiveness to all who confess their sin, believe in the sacrificial death of Jesus Christ, and accept Christ's payment.

What encouraging news to know that God has made a provision for each of us to have a completely new spiritual nature! What encouraging news that God does not hold our sins against us once we have received forgiveness! He forgets our past and makes *all* things new for us. If you encounter people who are suffering under guilt or can't seem to let go of their past, give them the good news: "God wants to forgive you and give you a new life in Christ Jesus!"

꙳ List three people whom you can encourage this week with the news of God's forgiveness. When will you share this news with each?

꙰

Three Lies that Keep People from Forgiveness

Satan is the father of all lies, and some of his foremost lies relate to God's forgiveness. Above all else, Satan does not want a person to receive God's forgiveness or to be given the gifts of a new nature and eternal life. Three of his lies are these:

1. You are a good person, and therefore you do not need to be forgiven.

2. Your sins are too great, too horrible, to be forgiven.

3. Your sins have been repeated too often to be forgiven.

∞ Every Person Needs Forgiveness ∞

Satan's first lie is usually an attempt to convince a person that he doesn't *need* salvation. He whispers to the heart, "You're OK. You haven't done anything wrong. Everybody makes mistakes. In fact, in comparison to other people, you haven't done anything all that bad."

God's Word says that every person is in need of forgiveness. We all are born with a sin nature that is in need of being changed (Romans 3:23). We all fail to keep God's commandments—sometimes out of ignorance, and sometimes willfully and rebelliously. To claim that we don't have a sin nature or that we do not sin is sheer folly (1 John 1:6, 8). God does not grade "on a curve." He judges the nature of mankind as being either forgiven or unforgiven. You cannot be good enough, or do enough good deeds, to earn God's forgiveness. God's forgiveness is always a gift, never something that we can achieve by our own efforts (Ephesians 2:8–9).

Sometimes a person will suffer with guilt and shame, and yet attempt to justify their position by saying, "But I don't deserve this guilt and shame. I'm a *good person.*" The most loving and encouraging thing that you can say is this: "Sin results in our feeling guilt, shame, and a sense of being 'unclean.' But God has made a way for each of us to be free from the weight of sin!" The news that we don't need to earn our own salvation is a blessed relief. Accepting God's forgiveness is an easy act. It is an act of humbly receiving, not an act of earning or achieving.

For all have sinned and fall short of the glory of God.

—Romans 3:23

๛ What does it mean to "fall short of the glory of God"?

๛ What is the "good news" which goes along with this "bad news"? How can you use this "good news/bad news" this week to encourage someone?

∞ No Sin Too Great ∞

Many people are locked into this lie of Satan: "You have done something so terrible that it is beyond God's forgiveness." God's Word declares that no person is beyond God's love and forgiveness, regardless of what they have done! We only need to take a brief look at the Word of God to see that God forgave:

🙿 **Abraham and Sarah**, who missed God's perfect plan for their lives, the result being an illegitimate child

🙿 **Moses**, who committed murder

🙿 **David**, who committed adultery **and** murder

🙿 **Peter**, who denied knowing Jesus three times, in the time of Jesus' greatest suffering

🙿 **Paul**, who persecuted Christians and was responsible for their deaths

God had a plan for the redemption and complete reconciliation of each of these great leaders in the Bible. His plan for redemption through Jesus Christ is offered to all today, regardless of their past sins. All sin is equal before God. In other words, there are no bad sins, not-so-bad sins, and only-a-little-bad sins. Sin doesn't exist by degree. Sin is sin. Sin stains the spirit regardless of its "type" or "size."

God's offer of forgiveness covers *all* sin. No variety or dimension of sin is beyond His loving capacity for forgiveness.

> Blessed are those whose lawless deeds are forgiven, and whose sins are covered; blessed is the man to whom the Lord shall not impute sin.
>
> —Romans 4:7-8

🙿 Your sins "are covered" in the sense of being buried in the grave. What does this suggest about God's forgiveness?

31

∞ God's Mercy Cannot Be Exhausted ∞

Some people believe that they have exhausted God's mercy through repeated sinful acts after their salvation. Satan has fed them the lie: "You have known God's forgiveness, and now look, you are sinning again. God's fed up with you. He's not going to continue to forgive you time after time."

God's Word says that God has "abundant mercy" (1 Peter 1:3). We cannot exhaust His supply of forgiveness. Each time we sin, we are to come to God and ask for His forgiveness, and then receive His forgiveness and to ask for His help, that we might not sin again as we have. What good news to know that we can be forgiven, regardless of our past! If you encounter people who believe that they have put themselves outside the realm of God's forgiveness, share the encouraging truth of God: "You can *still* be forgiven! You are not beyond God's ability to forgive you. Your past does not need to be your future."

> For God so loved the world that He gave His only begotten Son, that whoever believes in Him should not perish but have everlasting life.
>
> —John 3:16

∾ Why is this verse a cause for rejoicing? How often do *you* rejoice in your salvation?

∾ How can this verse help you find encouragement this week?

And the grace of our Lord was exceedingly abundant, with faith and love which are in Christ Jesus.

—1 Timothy 1:14

❧ Why does Paul say that God's grace is "exceedingly abundant"? Why not just "abundant"?

❧ What does this suggest about God's ability to forgive?

Though your sins are like scarlet, They shall be as white as snow; Though they are red like crimson, They shall be as wool.

—Isaiah 1:18

❧ What is the worst sin, in your opinion, that you have ever committed? Was this sin covered and made "white as snow" by Christ's blood?

❧ How does this encourage you? How can you use this truth to encourage others this week?

❧ Today and Tomorrow ☙

Today: God forgives *and* forgets—but only as much as I forgive others.

Tomorrow: This week, I will spend time with God deliberately forgiving others who have wronged me.

❧ Notes and Prayer Requests: ❧

LESSON 4

You Are a Citizen of Heaven

☙ In This Lesson ❧

LEARNING: HOW CAN I BE SURE THAT TOMORROW WILL BE BETTER THAN TODAY?

GROWING: HOW DOES MY SALVATION BRING ENCOURAGEMENT TO SOMEONE ELSE?

You are heaven-bound! That's the encouraging news to every person who has believed in Jesus Christ and received God's forgiveness. Jesus said, "For God so loved the world that He gave His only begotten Son, *that whoever believes in Him should not perish but have everlasting life*" (John 3:16, emphasis added). A person gains two things the instant he accepts Christ into his life: eternal life, and an everlasting heavenly home.

Throughout the New Testament, we have numerous references to our heavenly home and to eternal life. Even so, a significant number of Christians struggle and are discouraged about their spiritual state and about their future. They question whether they are truly saved. They wonder if they will go to heaven when they die.

In this lesson, we will deal first with our assurance of salvation and the gift of everlasting life in heaven. Then, we will deal with how we are to live daily "in the hope of heaven."

Assurance of Eternal Life and a Heavenly Home

Those who believe that they somehow can "lose" their salvation once they have believed in Jesus Christ tend also to believe that they had something to do with gaining their salvation in the first place. The fact is, you did absolutely *nothing* to warrant your salvation—to earn it, achieve it, or to be worthy of it. Your salvation was a gift of God, extended to you by His mercy and out of His fathomless love, made possible through the shed blood of Jesus Christ on the cross. The initiative for your salvation was God's. It was God through His Spirit who convicted you of your sin and wooed you to Christ Jesus. It is God who saved you and then filled you with His Holy Spirit. It is God who promised you eternal life. And it is God who will bring you to the fullness of a life with Him in heaven.

The Bible refers to Jesus as the "author" of your faith—and also the "finisher" of your faith (Heb. 12:2). The good work that He has started in you, He is committed to completing! (1 Thessalonians 5:24). In like manner, there is absolutely *nothing* that you can do to "undo" your salvation. Just as a baby cannot return to the womb after he has been born, so you cannot return to your old sin nature once you have been born again spiritually. Your nature has been changed.

Romans 10:9–10 tells us, "If you confess with your mouth the Lord Jesus and believe in your heart that God has raised Him from the dead, you will be saved. For with the heart one believes unto righteousness, and with the mouth confession is made unto salvation."

If you have any doubt today about your salvation, go to God, acknowledge that your sinful nature has separated you from Him, believe in what Jesus did for you on the cross, and confess your faith in Jesus Christ. Receive His forgiveness, and then have faith that you are saved! You are a child of God forever, fully reconciled and justified before Him.

He who believes in the Son has everlasting life; and he who does not believe the Son shall not see life, but the wrath of God abides on him.

—John 3:36

‌ Have you accepted Christ as your Savior, asking Him to forgive you of your sins?

‌ Do you sometimes wonder whether you are truly saved? What causes these doubts? How does this verse prove that a person is eternally saved once he accepts Christ's salvation?

‌ Absent from the Flesh, Present with the Lord ‌

The understanding of the apostles was clear: Death is not an end point for the believer but merely a transition into the direct presence of the Lord. Paul wrote to the Corinthians that "to be absent from the body" is to be "present with the Lord" (2 Corinthians 5:6–8).

Paul also described death merely as a "change" (1 Corinthians 15:52–54). We move in a moment's time from living in a temporary physical body on a physical earth to living in a glorified body in our eternal home (1 Corinthians 15:42–44).

37

Behold, I tell you a mystery: We shall not all sleep, but we shall all be changed in a moment, in the twinkling of an eye, at the last trumpet. For the trumpet will sound, and the dead will be raised incorruptible, and we shall be changed. For this corruptible must put on incorruption, and this mortal must put on immortality.

—1 Corinthians 15:51-53

❧ What does Paul mean when he says that "this mortal must put on immortality"?

❧ In what ways will you be "changed" when you stand in heaven before God?

∞ Our Coming Resurrection ∞

The writers of the New Testament spoke frequently about our coming resurrection, which is made possible by the resurrection of Jesus Christ. In fact, the writer of Hebrews stated that the "resurrection of the dead" is one of the elementary principles of Christ (Hebrews 6:1–2).

Jesus said of Himself, "I am the resurrection and the life. He who believes in Me, though he may die, he shall live. And whoever lives and believes in Me shall never die" (John 11:25–26). The apostle Paul taught that we shall be raised from death as Christ was raised, just as we have been crucified with Him (Romans 6:5, 8–9).

> Now if we died with Christ, we believe that we shall also live with Him, knowing that Christ, having been raised from the dead, dies no more. Death no longer has dominion over Him.
>
> —Romans 6:8-9

❧ What does it mean that "death no longer has dominion" over Christ? What does this imply about your own eternal life?

❧ In what way does a person "die with Christ"? How does this relationship secure your own eternal life?

39

⊸ Promises to the Overcomer ⊸

Those who stay true to Jesus Christ and follow Him to the best of their ability will be those whom the Holy Spirit helps to overcome sin and evil. And what a promise lies ahead for those who overcome! John cited a number of these:

- to eat from the tree of life (Revelation 2:7)

- to receive the crown of life (Revelation 2:10)

- to be clothed in white garments (Revelation 3:5)

- to receive a new name (Revelation 3:12)

- to sit with Jesus on His throne (Revelation 3:21)

Our eternal life will be marked by rewards and everlasting blessings.

⊸ Our Heavenly Home ⊸

Jesus wanted His disciples to be assured that they would have a heavenly home. He comforted them in John 14:1–4, 6:

Let not your heart be troubled; you believe in God, believe also in Me. In My Father's house are many mansions; if it were not so, I would have told you. I go to prepare a place for you. And if I go and prepare a place for you, I will come again and receive you to Myself; that where I am there you may be also. And where I go you know, and the way you know ... I am the way, the truth, and the life. No one comes to the Father except through Me.

Jesus is preparing a heavenly home for us, and He has provided the means for us to enter into that home. And what a glorious place our heavenly home is going to be! John described it as a place where all things will be made new and where there will be no more sorrow, suffering, or pain. We will live in the everlasting presence of God (Revelation 21:3–5).

God has a wonderful future planned for the true believer in Christ Jesus. Those who are elderly and those who are seriously ill *especially* need to hear the encouraging word of eternal life and a heavenly home. Be quick to share God's Word with all who are suffering or who may be near death.

> And God will wipe away every tear from their eyes; there shall be no more death, nor sorrow, nor crying. There shall be no more pain, for the former things have passed away.
>
> —Revelation 21:4

What "tears" do you want God to "wipe away"?

Who can you encourage with this good news with this week?

Living in the Hope of Heaven

We are challenged repeatedly in God's Word to live "in the hope of heaven." Heaven is to be at the forefront of our thinking. It is to be our constant anticipation, an active and lively hope. This hope works in three ways:

1. We have a renewed desire to abstain from evil and pursue righteousness, as well as a new appreciation for all things eternal.

2. We have a new desire to witness to others about Christ Jesus.

3. We experience great joy about the future.

⤜ A Focus on the Eternal ⤜

The person who has his eyes on a heavenly home will do everything within his power to abstain from evil and embrace what God calls good. There is a new focus on the things of God and a stripping away from anything that might detract.

Along with this new alignment of priorities, the person with an active hope of heaven has a renewed energy and enthusiasm for all things that are eternal. There is a new ability to see that some trials and troubles in this life are only for a "little while." In the context of eternity, many things suddenly appear trivial or momentary.

There is also a renewed interest in the Word of God, which endures forever, and in associating with those who believe in the Word of God.

Therefore we also, since we are surrounded by so great a cloud of witnesses, let us lay aside every weight, and the sin which so easily ensnares us, and let us run with endurance the race that is set before us.

—Hebrews 12:1

❧ What sins do you find yourself "easily ensnared" by? How will you resolve to gain victory this week?

❧ What "race" has God "set before you" this week? How will you run that race with endurance?

❧ A Desire to Witness About Christ ❧

The person who has a living, active hope about heaven will want to produce as much eternal "fruit" as possible, especially the winning of lost souls. The person who truly believes in a heavenly home will want as many people as possible to enter heaven with him!

Go therefore and make disciples of all the nations, baptizing them in the name of the Father and of the Son and of the Holy Spirit, teaching them to observe all things that I have commanded you; and lo, I am with you always, even to the end of the age." Amen.

—Matthew 28:19-20

∾ When have you shared the gospel with someone who didn't know Christ? Did you find it encouraging?

∾ List one or two people that you can tell about Christ this week.

∾ **Joy About the Future** ∾

The person who has an active, living hope about heaven has an exuberance of joy. There is a delight in knowing that God is at work and that we shall one day experience the fullness of His work in us. There is a joy in *knowing* that we will *always* have a tomorrow in which to love and serve our Creator!

So we are always confident, knowing that while we are at home in the body we are absent from the Lord. For we walk by faith, not by sight. We are confident, yes, well pleased rather to be absent from the body and to be present with the Lord.

—2 Corinthians 5:6-8

44

❧ What does it mean to "walk by faith, not by sight"? Give practical examples.

❧ Why would Paul be "well pleased" to die? What does this suggest about the things that seem important in this life?

> For since by man came death, by Man also came the resurrection of the dead. For as in Adam all die, even so in Christ all shall be made alive.
>
> —1 Corinthians 15:21-22

❧ Explain, in your own words, how death came into the world "by man".

❧ Explain how "in Adam all die". You cannot be "unborn" from Adam's lineage. What does this suggest about your eternal security once you are "born again" into Christ's lineage?

> For now we see in a mirror, dimly, but then face to face. Now I know in part, but then I shall know just as I also am known.
>
> —1 Corinthians 13:12

❧ What does it mean that "now we see in a mirror, dimly"? What aspects of life do we see dimly at times?

❧ How would you feel if you could see Jesus today "face to face"? How might you be encouraged knowing that you had an appointment with Him tomorrow morning?

Therefore, since all these things will be dissolved, what manner of persons ought you to be in holy conduct and godliness, looking for and hastening the coming of the day of God...?

—2 Peter 3:11-12

☙ Answer Peter's question in your own words: What sort of person ought *you* to be "in holy conduct and godliness"?

☙ Today and Tomorrow ☙

TODAY: I WILL FIND THE GREATEST ENCOURAGEMENT BY BEING IN OBEDIENCE TO CHRIST.

TOMORROW: I WILL SHARE THE GOOD NEWS OF ETERNITY WITH SOMEONE ELSE THIS WEEK.

LESSON 5

God Is in Control

─── ❧ **In This Lesson** ☙ ───

LEARNING: WHY DON'T I SEE GOD WORKING IN MY LIFE?

GROWING: HOW CAN I LEARN TO TRUST HIM MORE FULLY?

∞

One of the most encouraging verses in the entire Bible is Romans 8:28:

> And we know that all things work together for good to those who love God, to those who are the called according to His purpose.

This verse assures us that God is involved in every moment of our lives and that He is always at work to bring about His good and eternal purposes for us. The question nearly always arises, however, "If a good God is involved in all things, why do bad things happen?" Why does a spouse abandon a marriage? Why does a child use drugs? Why does a person lose a job?

We can feel discouraged if we dwell on the negative. Ultimately, we may begin to think, "What difference does it make if I follow God?" Let me say three things as we begin this lesson:

1. *God is involved in all things*. He simply can't be separated from any aspect of life since He is the creator, sustainer, and orchestrator of all that is. He is actively involved in all details of His creation.

2. *God has given mankind free will*. You have been made in the image of God, and part of His image is that you have freedom of choice. It is out of mankind's freedom of choice that Adam sinned. The result of his sin is that all of us are born with a tendency to choose sin. We have an inbred sin nature.

Much of the evil that occurs in our world today is rooted in our free will. A spouse *chooses* to abandon the marriage. The child *chooses* drugs. The company *chooses* to lay off employees.

Sometimes our choices are made unconsciously. A person may not choose to bring on a life-threatening disease, but years and years of choosing to live in certain ways with certain habits sometimes result in disease. A person may not choose indebtedness or financial setback, but years and years of overextending or of not saving may result in a financial crisis.

In still other instances, the "choices" that govern our lives are collective ones over which we have no personal control. We live in a world that is crime-ridden and war-torn. The fault lies with no one person and is not the result of one, singular choice. The collective "whole" of mankind's free will has simply gone amok, and individuals are victims of a fallen world.

God will not override free will. Most people want God to stay out of their lives—until they need Him—and God does not impose Himself on anyone. But this does not mean that God is absent. God is present in the midst of our bad choices. He is *with* us in our times of trouble, doubt, and struggle. He is always at work on our behalf, desiring our ultimate and eternal best. His Holy Spirit will continue to woo us to an acceptance of Christ and an opening of our heart to God's love.

Furthermore, we must recognize that sin has consequences. God does not promise that we will not reap what we sowed into our lives prior to our coming to Him. What He does promise is that He will use all things for our good and that He will prepare us to spend eternity with Him. God does not override our free will or negate the choices that we make with our free will.

3. *God's ultimate purposes will be accomplished.* In the end, God will have His way. His will *shall* be done. None of us is capable of seeing the big picture of God's plan because it extends into eternity. God alone knows what He has planned and how He intends to accomplish His master plan.

We can be certain of one thing, however: God will remain omnipotent, omniscient, and omnipresent. His nature will not change. He will always have the *power* to do what He desires. He will always *know* precisely what to do to accomplish His purposes. He will always have sufficient *time* to accomplish His purposes.

We may rebel against God's purposes, balk at His laws, disobey His commandments, and stubbornly refuse His forgiveness. Nevertheless, what God has planned, God will do. The decision that we face is this: Will we get in line with God's plan, or will we rebel against it?

I know that You can do everything, And that no purpose of Yours can be withheld from You.

—Job 42:2

๛ What is God's ultimate purpose for all His children? How can you see Him working out that purpose in your own life?

๛ When have you seen God take something unpleasant and turn it to something good in your own life?

Our Response to God Determines Our Outcome

This is the response that we must give continually in our lives: *I choose to yield the control of my life fully to God.* Yielding control to God is a response that we must make in every area of our lives; we must not withhold anything. We must yield control of our time, our energy, our money, our dreams, and our total selves. Our surrender to Him must be a complete surrender. God is in *all* things and His purposes will ultimately be accomplished, but He will only take control of all areas of our lives if we ask Him to do so.

Two people cannot hold the wheel of an automobile without disaster. One alone must be the driver. The same is true in our lives. We must give control to God and invite Him to be the driving force and direction of our lives. The Bible refers to this as submission (James 4:7). It is regarded as a "sacrifice" of oneself to God (Romans 12:1).

51

I beseech you therefore, brethren, by the mercies of God, that you present your bodies a living sacrifice, holy, acceptable to God, which is your reasonable service.

—Romans 12:1

∞ How do you feel about God's command to submit your entire life to His control? What areas do you find it most difficult to yield?

∞ Why does Paul beseech us "by the mercies of God"? How do God's mercies make a claim on your obedience?

∞ Consult God *Always* ∞

A person who has totally yielded his life to Christ Jesus will consult God about His will *at* all times, *about* all things, and *in* all situations. God is in control of the daily details of our lives only to the extent that we ask Him, "What do You want me to do?" No situation, circumstance, or relationship is beyond God's caring. He desires to impart to us His wisdom, answers, and solutions.

Yielding to God is not something that we do only once at the time we are saved. It is something that we do continually for the rest of our lives. It is an active *consulting* of God in all things.

> Seek the LORD while He may be found, Call upon Him while He is near. Let the wicked forsake his way, And the unrighteous man his thoughts; Let him return to the LORD, And He will have mercy on him; And to our God, For He will abundantly pardon.
>
> —Isaiah 55:6-7

When was the last time that you asked God for advice concerning a decision or problem? What was the result?

∽ Trust God in Methods and Timing ∽

God does not always manifest "control" *when* or *how* we think He should. God, however, knows precisely which method to use in which circumstance. He knows what is best for each life, and our role is to trust Him implicitly. God speaks to each of us in a voice that we can understand. He acts in each of our lives in a way that causes us to confront our lives and to see Him clearly. God will always impart His will to us in ways that we can comprehend.

In the broader scope of life, however, we are not always told what methods God is going to use. We do not know what God will choose to do to convict a lost sinner of his sin. We do not know what God will do to soften a hardened heart or to alter a rebellious course. We are to adopt a position of trust: God knows, and God will act when and how He chooses to act. His purposes are always for good, and so are His methods and His timing.

Even when we know that God is in control, we must always wait for Him to act *in His timing.* If God reveals to us what He is going to do, it is so that we might be ready to respond when He acts—not so that we can jump ahead of God and exact His justice or extend His mercy prior to His timetable. We err greatly anytime we get ahead of God or attempt to take matters of justice into our own hands.

Our prayer must always be, "Not my will, but Yours. Not my method, but Yours. Not my timing, but Yours." We must also recognize at all times that God is concerned about all of His children. He acts in ways that are beneficial to each of His beloved ones. Sometimes the will of God is delayed so that more souls may be saved, or even so that one particular lost sheep may be found.

As we trust God to act in the lives of others, we are to have a spirit of expectancy. We are to *look* for God at work, and we are to praise Him equally for His long-suffering, His execution of judgment, and His granting of mercy.

☙ Do you feel that God is being slow or even unresponsive in some area of your life? How will you work this week to trust Him more?

The LORD is righteous in all His ways, Gracious in all His works. The LORD is near to all who call upon Him, To all who call upon Him in truth.

—Psalm 145:17-18

❧ What does it mean to call upon God "in truth"? Do you generally call upon Him in truth, or do you sometimes have mixed motives?

❧ How can these verses help you this week to trust God's timing more fully?

The Encouraging Word

Some of the most encouraging statements that you can share with another person are these:

> ✍ God is in control of the situation, and He will accomplish His purposes.

> ✍ You can put yourself on God's side—the side of victory.

> ✍ You can trust God to act in precisely the right timing and method to accomplish the ultimate good in any situation.

This world is under the influence of the devil, but it is not under his control. God is in control—now and always.

Pause for a few moments to reflect upon the awesome power of God, and then answer these questions:

✍ Have you yielded full control for your life to God? Are you trusting God to exert control on a daily basis in your life?

✍ How are you being challenged in your role as one of God's encouragers? Is the Lord directing you to share the encouraging word that "God is in control" with a specific person?

Draw near to God and He will draw near to you. Cleanse your hands, you sinners; and purify your hearts, you double-minded.

—James 4:8

≈ In what areas do you tend to be "double-minded"? How, in practical terms, can you purify your heart this week?

≈ What does it mean to "draw near to God"? Give practical examples of how this is done.

O God, You are my God; Early will I seek You; My soul thirsts for You; My flesh longs for You In a dry and thirsty land Where there is no water.

—Psalms 63:1

✎ When have you genuinely felt this "longing" and "thirst" for God's presence in your life? How did that longing affect your life in general?

✎ In the past month, have you been "seeking God early"? Or have you tended to seek Him "late"? What will you do this week to seek Him early?

✎ Today and Tomorrow ✎

TODAY: GOD WILL ALWAYS HONOR MY FREE WILL, AND IT'S UP TO ME TO KEEP MY WILL IN LINE WITH HIS.

TOMORROW: I WILL PRAYERFULLY EXAMINE MY OWN LIFE THIS WEEK, STRIVING TO SUBMIT MYSELF FULLY TO GOD.

LESSON 6

God Will Enable You

✆ In This Lesson ✆

LEARNING: WHAT IS THE ROLE OF THE HOLY SPIRIT?

GROWING: HOW DOES HE AFFECT MY LIFE?

For many Christians, life is a matter of simply doing their best. They experience no power and no sense of victory in their souls. A humdrum spiritual life leads to discouragement. A spiritual life without a sense of progress, growth, and development can become tedious and wearisome.

Such a life, however, is *not* what God desires for us. The Bible holds out the promise of the Holy Spirit, who indwells us to enable us, equip us, and help us to lead an abundant, vibrant, purposeful life.

The Promise of the Spirit

Jesus promised His disciples, "I will not leave you as orphans; I will come to you" (John 14:18 NASB). He further promised, "I tell you the truth, it is to your advantage that I go away; for if I do not go away, the Helper shall not come to you; but if I go, I will send Him to you" (John 16:7 NASB). Just before His ascension into heaven, Jesus said, "You shall be baptized with the Holy Spirit not many days from now...you shall receive power when the Holy Spirit has come upon you" (Acts 1:5, 8 NASB).

The promise of the Holy Spirit is for all who believe. Those who confessed Jesus as Lord in the New Testament were filled with the Holy Spirit. The presence of the Holy Spirit is made available to all. Salvation requires that we receive the forgiveness of God *by faith*, and submitting to the Holy Spirit is also an act of faith.

The Holy Spirit dwells with us. He does not "come and go;" He resides within our spirits on a permanent basis. The frequent image used by the writers of the New Testament is that we are a temple of God, filled with the Spirit of God.

> Do you not know that you are the temple of God and that the Spirit of God dwells in you?
>
> —1 Corinthians 3:16

❧ What does it mean that "you are the temple of God"? How does this fact encourage you today?

The Work of the Holy Spirit in Us

The Holy Spirit operates within us on a daily basis to help us in all practical matters of Christian living. Specifically, the Holy Spirit works in the following ways:

He convicts us of sin and makes us aware when we are breaking God's commandments (John 16:8–11).

He illuminates the Word of God to us, helping us to understand and apply what we read in the Bible (John 16:12–15).

He teaches us the truth about God and the truth about ourselves (John 16:12–15).

He guides us into right decisions and choices, and into service and ministry (Rom. 8:14).

He assures us that we are born again and are the children of God, and that we are heirs with Christ of all God's promises and blessings (Romans 8:16).

He frees us from the bondage of fear (Romans 8:15).

He intercedes on our behalf, always praying the will of God for us (Romans 8:26).

He arms us with the whole armor of God, preparing us for spiritual warfare (Acts 20:23).

In our daily battle against the temptations of this world, the Holy Spirit prompts us continually about what is right and wrong. We do not have the role model of Jesus on the earth today to be a living picture for us about how to live, so the Holy Spirit reveals to us the right way. The Holy Spirit also equips us to fight and defeat the enemy of our souls. He assures us that we have victory over an already-judged, already-defeated foe (John 16:11). His presence in us is active constantly. He is always seeking our highest and best good, now and for all eternity.

> However, when He, the Spirit of truth, has come, He will guide
> you into all truth....

> —John 16:13

> When has the Holy Spirit "guided you into truth"?

> Why is He called "the Spirit of truth"? What does this suggest about the ways in which He will guide you?

∞ **Creation of Our New Identity** ∞

The Holy Spirit works within us to create a new character or identity in us. Our new nature is marked by these characteristics (Galatians 5:22-23):

꙼ *Love* for those who do not love in return.

꙼ *Joy*, even in the midst of painful circumstances.

꙼ *Peace* when something that we were counting on doesn't come through.

꙼ *Long-suffering* when things aren't going fast enough for us.

꙼ *Kindness* toward those who treat us unkindly or have rejected us.

꙼ *Goodness* toward those who have sought to do us harm.

꙼ *Faithfulness* when friends have proved unfaithful.

꙼ *Gentleness* toward those who deal harshly with us and persecute us for no just cause.

꙼ *Self-control* in the face of intense temptation.

Conversely, the Holy Spirit strips away from us the old characteristics that we exhibited before we received God's Spirit, chiseling at us bit by bit, sanding away our sinful habits and the hard edges of our personalities. He causes us to put away our former behaviors—deeds that Paul calls "works of the flesh"—such as "adultery, fornication, uncleanness, licentiousness, idolatry, sorcery, hatred, contentions, jealousies, outbursts of wrath, selfish ambitions, dissensions, heresies, envy, murders, drunkenness, revelries, and the like" (Galians 5:19–21a).

The new character traits that the Holy Spirit produces in us are called the "fruit of the Spirit". They are the very character traits that marked Jesus' life! Indeed, the Holy Spirit is "Christ in us." The apostle Paul wrote in Galatians 2:20, "I have been crucified with Christ; it is no longer I who live, but Christ lives in me; and the life which I now live in the flesh I live by faith in the Son of God, who loved me and gave Himself for me."

> But now having been set free from sin, and having become slaves of God, you have your fruit to holiness, and the end, everlasting life.
>
> —Romans 6:22

⚘ Give real-life examples of "fruit to holiness". Which of these fruit are apparent in your life? Which ones need more cultivation?

∞ Ability to Stand Against the Devil ∞

The Holy Spirit's presence in us gives us the ability to say "no" to the devil's temptations and lies, and also the ability to withstand the devil's assaults on our life.

> Likewise you also, reckon yourselves to be dead indeed to sin, but alive to God in Christ Jesus our Lord. Therefore do not let sin reign in your mortal body, that you should obey it in its lusts. And do not present your members as instruments of unrighteousness to sin, but present yourselves to God as being alive from the dead, and your members as instruments of righteousness to God.

> —Romans 6:11-13

℞ If your body were literally dead, how would temptations be different? How can you learn to "reckon yourself to be dead indeed to sin"?

℞ Give practical examples of ways in which people present their "members as instruments of unrighteousness". How would your own life be different if you always presented yourself to God "as being alive from the dead"?

∾ Ability to Witness About Christ Jesus ∾

The first and foremost sign of the Holy Spirit's presence in a person's life is the power to give witness to Christ Jesus (Acts 1:8). We are called to present Christ to others—in our words as well as our deeds.

> Let your light so shine before men, that they may see your good works and glorify your Father in heaven.
>
> —Matthew 5:16

🕭 Give practical examples of what it means to "let your light shine before men".

🕭 When have you been moved to glorify God because of someone's godly lifestyle? When has your own life affected someone else that way?

Our Daily Walk in the Spirit

God calls us to "walk in the Spirit" (Galatians 5:16, 25). We do this when we ask the Holy Spirit daily for guidance in all that we do: at the time of each major decision, in the face of each new problem, in the course of each conversation. We must learn to listen to the voice of the Spirit speaking in us. As we do, the Holy Spirit becomes an ever-present source of encouragement to us.

The person who lives in boldness and joy does so because he knows that:

    ∾ he has the assurance of eternal life

    ∾ he cannot fail if he obeys God's commands

    ∾ he will receive the full provision and protection of the Holy Spirit until his mission in life is fulfilled

The Holy Spirit is the Encourager who lives within. He is the Enabler of the abundant life that Jesus promised us when He said, "The thief does not come except to steal, and to kill, and to destroy. I have come that they may have life, and that they may have it more abundantly" (John 10:10).

> But if the Spirit of Him who raised Jesus from the dead dwells in you, He who raised Christ from the dead will also give life to your mortal bodies through His Spirit who dwells in you.
>
> —Romans 8:11

∾ How do you know that, as a Christian, the Holy Spirit dwells within you? Cite Scripture passages to support your answer.

∾ What does this verse promise concerning your eternal future? What does it suggest about the Holy Spirit's function in your life today?

> Likewise the Spirit also helps in our weaknesses. For we do not know what we should pray for as we ought, but the Spirit Himself makes intercession for us with groanings which cannot be uttered.
>
> —Romans 8:26

❧ When has God's Spirit helped you in your weaknesses in the past? How might He help you more in the coming week?

❧ What does it mean that the Holy Spirit "makes intercession for us with groanings which cannot be uttered"? How does that knowledge comfort and encourage you?

LESSON 6

For you did not receive the spirit of bondage again to fear, but you received the Spirit of adoption by whom we cry out, "Abba, Father."

—Romans 8:15

❧ "Abba" is similar to "daddy". Have you ever prayed to God, calling Him "daddy"?

❧ How does God's Spirit free us from "bondage" to fear? What things are you presently fearing in life? How can the Spirit set you free?

Therefore take up the whole armor of God, that you may be able to withstand in the evil day, and having done all, to stand.

—Ephesians 6:13

Read also verses 14-18. Describe each article of the "armor of God". What does each piece of armor protect? What is required for that armor to be effective?

How does this apply to our practical work in fighting against the devil?

Today and Tomorrow

Today: The Holy Spirit strips away my sinful nature, and gives me a new Christ-like nature.

Tomorrow: This week, I will ask God to help me live more fully in His Spirit.

LESSON 7

You Can Live in Freedom

☙ In This Lesson ❧

LEARNING: WHY ARE THERE SOME AREAS OF SIN THAT SEEM TO MAKE ME A SLAVE?

GROWING: HOW CAN I GAIN TRUE FREEDOM IN CHRIST?

Freedom! What a wonderful word to us. We all value freedom highly. We delight in being free. We long to live in freedom always.

One of the most encouraging themes in the New Testament is that Christians are free in Christ Jesus. This especially was good news to the Christians who first received this teaching from the apostles, since many were slaves. The freedom that the apostles spoke about, however, was not a political freedom but a spiritual one. They spoke of an inner freedom that allows a person to live above his present circumstances.

This is a freedom that is no less important in our world today, when many people feel trapped in the bondage of addictions, depression, abusive relationships, and other oppressive situations. The world in which we live is not godly, and we must experience the freedom that Christ offers to us so that we can live in the world, yet not be "of" the world.

The Foundation of Our Freedom

Our freedom in Christ is directly related to two main concepts in the Bible:

- *Redemption*: we have been redeemed by Christ Jesus.

- *Service*: we are destined to serve one of two masters.

The choice to receive Christ brings about our redemption and puts us into the service of God. A failure to receive Christ keeps a person from experiencing redemption and keeps him in servitude to the "law of sin and death."

∞ Redemption ∞

The word *redemption* in the Greek and Roman culture literally referred to the purchase of a slave from the marketplace, with the purpose of giving the slave his freedom. In spiritual terms, the word means that the blood of Jesus paid the "ransom" that was required for each of us to be set free from our sin nature and experience the fullness of God's forgiveness and love. God provided a total means of redemption through the death of Jesus on the cross. Revelation 5:9 tells us about Jesus, "You were slain, and have redeemed us to God by Your blood out of every tribe and tongue and people and nation."

Jesus taught His disciples that His very purpose was to provide redemption. He said, "The Son of Man did not come to be served, but to serve, and to give His life a ransom for many" (Matthew 20:28, Mark 10:45). Paul also referred to the redemptive purpose of Jesus when he wrote, "There is one God and one Mediator between God and men, the Man Christ Jesus, who gave Himself a ransom for all" (1 Timothy 2:5–6a).

Redemption is not a concept limited to the New Testament. The message of redemption can be seen from cover to cover in the Bible: God planned our redemption (Genesis 1–2); God required redemption (Genesis 3:11); God prepared the way for redemption (Genesis 12 through Malachi); God instituted His redemptive plan through Jesus Christ (the Gospels); news of God's redemptive plan was spread (Acts); the redemptive plan was explained (the Epistles); and the redemption of man will be consummated (Revelation). The entire Bible is the story of God's redeeming love.

Our spiritual freedom has been purchased for us by God through His Son Jesus Christ. Just as no slave could redeem himself, so no person can redeem himself spiritually. We are indebted forever to the One who paid the price for our freedom, since there is no means by which we can pay Him back for what He has done for us. We are free from sin, yet we are not really free to do as we please. We have a great debt of gratitude; indeed, we owe our eternal lives to Christ Jesus, who purchased our freedom for us.

> He has delivered us from the power of darkness and conveyed us into the kingdom of the Son of His love, in whom we have redemption through His blood, the forgiveness of sins.
>
> —Colossians 1:13-14

❧ Before you were redeemed, what "powers of darkness" were you enslaved to? How has Christ's grace set you free?

73

∾ Service ∾

A second important concept related to our freedom is this: As human beings, we *will* serve one of two masters. We will either serve God and His system of righteousness or we will serve the devil and his system of evil. Romans 6:18 says, "Having been set free from sin, you became slaves of righteousness." Jesus said that no man can serve two masters simultaneously. We will serve either one or the other.

∾ The Nature of Our Freedom ∾

When we put these two concepts together, we come to the conclusion that we have been set free from the bondage of sin and death, *and* that we are set free to *serve* God in righteousness. Our freedom is not un-limited, unbridled freedom. Salvation is never a license to sin. Rather, our freedom is the freedom that allows us the great privilege to live above the world's systems and the law of sin and death. We no longer are enslaved to sinful passions, lusts, and desires. Instead, we are the bondservants of Christ.

> No one can serve two masters; for either he will hate the one and love the other, or else he will be loyal to the one and de-spise the other. You cannot serve God and mammon.
>
> —Matthew 6:24

∾ "Mammon" refers to the things of this world. How have you found in your own experience that you cannot fully serve both God and this world?

๛ What temptations of the world are still trying to enslave you? In what ways have you become a true "slave of God"?

Freedom from Temptation

No person is ever entirely free from temptation, but we can experience a release from a "season" or a siege of temptation. We see this in the life of Jesus when He was in the wilderness being tempted by the devil. The tempter came to Jesus with three rounds of temptation, and each time, Jesus refuted him with the Word of God. In the final round, Jesus commanded the devil, "Away with you, Satan! For it is written, 'You shall worship the LORD your God, and Him only you shall serve'" (Matthew 4:10). At that, the Bible tells us, "the devil left Him, and behold, angels came and ministered to Him" (v. 11). There was a definitive end to this season of temptation in Jesus' life.

This does not mean that Jesus was never tempted again. Rather, it means that Jesus functioned in full freedom as He conducted His ministry of preaching, teaching, and healing. The issue of His loyalty to God alone had been settled in a definitive way, and Jesus could never again be tempted on that point.

Each of us has a tendency to sin in certain ways. The devil knows that, and it is at our weakest point that he comes to tempt us—sometimes in a way that seems unrelenting. How can we experience freedom from his steady barrage of temptation? By using the same method that Jesus used: We can speak the Word of God every time that the tempter whispers his lies to us. For example:

 ✍ When the devil tells us that we are weak, we can declare, "God says that I am strong" (Joel 3:10).

 ✍ When the devil says that we are doomed to failure, we can declare, "God says that I am more than a conqueror" (Romans 8:37).

 ✍ When the devil says that we can never change, we can declare, "God says that I am a new creature in Christ Jesus" (2 Corinthians 5:17).

 ✍ When the devil says that we are not worthy of God's love, we can declare, "God says that He loved me so much that He sent Jesus to die for my sins so that I might live with God forever!" (John 3:16).

Regardless of what temptation you may experience, God has provided a passage of His Word that declares such a temptation to be a lie of Satan. Find the portion of God's Word that applies to your specific circumstance and use it as a "sword of the Spirit" (Ephesians 6:17).

 ✍ What temptations do you face on a fairly regular basis? What does God's word say about this temptation?

Therefore submit to God. Resist the devil and he will flee from you.

—James 4:7

☙ What does it mean to "resist the devil"? How did Jesus set the example of this when He was tempted?

☙ How can "submitting to God" help us to avoid temptation in the first place? Give practical examples.

The Role of Prayer. When faced with recurring temptation, we must also ask for the help of the Holy Spirit in withstanding the temptation. Jesus said that we are to pray, "Do not lead us into temptation"— in other words, do not allow us to get into situations in which we are subject to the devil's tempting (Matthew 6:13). On the night in which Jesus was betrayed, He had said to His disciples, "Watch and pray, lest you enter into temptation. The spirit indeed is willing, but the flesh is weak" (Matthew 26:41). We are to speak God's Word to the tempter and to ask God for strength *not* to yield to the devil's temptations.

All Are Tempted. Many people become discouraged when they still experience temptation after they are born again. The fact is, all people are tempted, for all of their lives. We are never beyond temptation.

We must be very clear on two points, however: 1) God does not tempt us to do evil just to see if we will yield. God has no association whatsoever with evil. 2) The Holy Spirit can help us withstand evil. We must never

77

attempt to justify our behavior by saying, "The devil made me do it" or "God made me this weak, so He knows that I couldn't help myself." The Holy Spirit is our strong ally in helping us withstand temptation. We can resist the devil and his lies. And the good news is that, when we resist the devil, he *will* flee from us (James 4:7).

> Blessed is the man who endures temptation; for when he has been approved, he will receive the crown of life which the Lord has promised to those who love Him.
>
> —James 1:12

☙ What does James mean by "when he has been approved"? What does this "approval" have to do with resisting temptation?

☙ What are some practical blessings or benefits to be gained by resisting temptation? What are some spiritual blessings? Give real-life examples of each.

∞ Deliverance ∞

In some cases, as discussed above, God asks us to use our will, to use His Word, and to rely upon the Holy Spirit to withstand temptation. In other cases, God chooses sovereignly to deliver us from evil and to wipe out the evil force that is coming against us.

Moses experienced this at the crossing of the Red Sea. He and the children of Israel were camped by the Red Sea and the enemy armies of Pharaoh were approaching rapidly to take them back into slavery—but the Lord gave these words to Moses (Exodus 14:13–14):

> "Do not be afraid. Stand still, and see the salvation of the LORD, which He will accomplish for you today. For the Egyptians whom you see today, you shall see again no more forever. The LORD will fight for you, and you shall hold your peace."

That is precisely what came to pass. The Lord opened up the Red Sea before Moses so that all the children of Israel could walk across on dry ground, and then He closed the waters on top of the entire army of Pharaoh. "Not so much as one of them remained" (Exodus 14:28b). God completely delivered the Israelites from this enemy. They still faced other enemies and other challenges, but Pharaoh and his army never came against them again.

Jesus had an active ministry of deliverance to those who were possessed or oppressed by the devil. Time and again, He rebuked the evil spirits that kept people in bondage. The spirits fled at His command and did not return. The deliverance was definitive and complete.

If you know a person who is in need of deliverance from an evil spirit, there are five things which they and you must do:

1. *Do not be afraid.* God tells us plainly that the Holy Spirit in us is greater than the devil of this world (1 John 4:4).

2. *Ask other believers to join with you in prayer and fasting.*

3. *Speak against the oppressing spirit in the name of Jesus.* There is no greater power on earth than the Name of Jesus; His name is higher than anything that attempts to rule over us (Philippians 2:9–10).

4. *Believe that God will act on your behalf.* Firmly put your trust in God and believe that He hears you and answers you (Psalm 91:14–15).

5. *Claim deliverance from a problem by faith, then immediately fill the void left behind that addiction, problem, or spirit.*

If the person's mind has been occupied with thoughts of evil, he must take all thoughts captive and turn his attention to God's Word and fill his mind with thoughts of righteousness. This is done by reading and studying God's Word, and by memorizing it (2 Corinthians 10:4–5). If the person's time has been spent in sinful activities, he must find something new and *righteous* to do. Time spent pursuing sin can be turned into time spent in prayer or in service to others. If the person has friends who are still dabbling in evil, he must find new friends. He must get involved in a Bible-believing church and stay involved. To fail to take a positive step forward is to invite evil to return (Matthew 12:43–45).

> Therefore God also has highly exalted Him and given Him the name which is above every name, that at the name of Jesus every knee should bow, of those in heaven, and of those on earth, and of those under the earth.
>
> —Philippians 2:9-10

80

☙ Who and what is under the power of Jesus' name, according to these verses? How does this help us when we are faced with the powers of darkness?

☙ Why is it vitally important that we name the name of Jesus when confronted with the powers of darkness? How does this compare with the fact that, in America today, the name of Jesus is effectively banned from most public situations (such as public schools)?

∞ Trust in God's Grace ∞

At still other times, the Lord provides freedom for us by giving us more of His grace to withstand the trial, rather than removing the trial from us. Paul experienced this. Three times he prayed and asked God to free him from what he called a "thorn in the flesh" that had been given to him as a "messenger of Satan." Rather than remove this thorn, however, the Lord said to Paul, "My grace is sufficient for you, for My strength is made perfect in weakness" (2 Corinthians 12:9a).

God's higher purpose—one of trust, a stronger faith, and a more potent witness—was worked in Paul's life. Paul came to the point where he declared, "I will rather boast in my infirmities, that the power of Christ may rest upon me...For when I am weak, then I am strong" (2 Corinthians 12:9b–10).

If God does not remove a temptation from you or does not deliver you sovereignly from an evil situation, He may very well be calling upon you to abide in His presence and to trust Him *in spite of* an evil situation or trial.

⁓ The Means Are up to God ⁓

We are not in a position to choose which means God might use to bring us into freedom in Christ Jesus. The encouraging news, however, is that the Lord promises us a "way out" of the evil that comes against us. He will not allow us to be tempted beyond our ability. He assures our redemption. We will not remain bound or captive to an evil situation, addiction, or relationship if we turn to Him and ask for His help.

꙳ When has God "freed" you from evil by giving you these three gifts: the power to withstand temptation; deliverance from evil; grace to trust God even more?

> No temptation has overtaken you except such as is common to man; but God is faithful, who will not allow you to be tempted beyond what you are able, but with the temptation will also make the way of escape, that you may be able to bear it.
>
> —1 Corinthians 10:13

꙳ When have you acted in faith on this verse, and discovered a way out of temptation that you hadn't seen before?

Two Freedoms that We Enjoy

As Christians, we enjoy freedom from the oppression of sin and evil, and we enjoy these two additional freedoms:

ॐ Freedom to fully know our purpose in living and to fulfill that purpose

ॐ Freedom to serve

These are freedoms that we must both claim by faith and pursue. They do not happen to us automatically, but they are ours for the asking.

∞ Freedom to Fulfill Our Purpose ∞

God has made each of us with unique talents and gifts which are to be used for a unique role in furthering His kingdom on earth. We are His workmanship, and He wants us to know the role for which we have been created (Ephesians 2:10). Ask God to reveal to you His purpose for your life. The person who discovers his talents and knows how God intends him to use them is not plagued by self-doubt or low self-esteem. There is great freedom in knowing that you are valuable and important to God and that He is guiding your steps and preparing you for even greater blessings.

ॐ Are you experiencing the freedom that comes from knowing who God created you to be and what He has called you to do? If not, how can you discover that freedom this week?

∞ Freedom to Serve Others ∞

When we know who we are in Christ Jesus, we experience a great freedom to serve others. We lose our self-conscious pride. We are willing to take risks in showing love to others. We know that we are saved and called to be God's people on the earth! The person who has his identity clearly in focus has very few emotional or spiritual barriers. He feels utterly free to speak *whatever* God leads him to speak, to do *whatever* God leads him to do, and to go *wherever* God leads.

The encouraging news is that God has work for you to do! He has someone who needs what you have to give. He has a purpose for you, and He wants you to be fulfilled in life.

> For you, brethren, have been called to liberty; only do not use liberty as an opportunity for the flesh, but through love serve one another.
>
> —Galatians 5:13

∞ When have you experienced a release from temptation by serving others?

∞ What people or ministries might God be calling you to serve this week?

Let no one say when he is tempted, "I am tempted by God"; for God cannot be tempted by evil, nor does He Himself tempt anyone. But each one is tempted when he is drawn away by his own desires and enticed. Then, when desire has conceived, it gives birth to sin; and sin, when it is full-grown, brings forth death.

—James 1:13-15

When have you tried to blame God or others for your own failure to resist temptation?

Notice James' metaphor of giving birth to sin. How is "desire" similar to a baby growing within the womb? What does this teach us about resisting temptation?

For the weapons of our warfare are not carnal but mighty in God for pulling down strongholds, casting down arguments and every high thing that exalts itself against the knowledge of God, bringing every thought into captivity to the obedience of Christ....

—2 Corinthians 10:4-5

🖎 What are some examples of "carnal weapons" that we sometimes use to fight temptation? What are examples of Godly weapons against temptation?

🖎 Give some practical examples from the world today of "every high thing that exalts itself against the knowledge of God". How can we combat this trend in the world today?

🖎 Today and Tomorrow 🖎

TODAY: BEING FREE IN CHRIST ALSO MEANS BECOMING HIS SERVANT, RATHER THAN A SLAVE TO SIN.

TOMORROW: THIS WEEK, I WILL MAKE IT A POINT TO SERVE OTHERS.

You Are Being Transformed

Every Christian is in the process of being changed, more and more, into the nature of Christ Jesus. Many books on the market today offer self-improvement, but they almost universally advocate that a person can change himself into the person that he wants to be. Intellectual and emotional growth are certainly possible in the natural realm, but *spiritual change* does not happen at the will of man.

A person who seeks to change himself spiritually believes that he will become a "better" person if he can just do more good deeds, learn more about God, or accomplish more for God's kingdom. This approach inevitably results in anxiety, frustration, discouragement, and perhaps even depression.

The encouraging news is that you cannot change yourself spiritually, but *God is in the process of changing you!* From the moment that you accept Jesus Christ as your Savior, you enter God's "change" process. Your spiritual transformation occurs at the initiative of God, and according to His timetable and methods.

The Bible tells us that we are being transformed in two ways:

1. We are being transformed by the renewal of our minds.

2. We are being conformed into the image of Christ.

In each case, the Holy Spirit is the "agent of the change" that occurs within us. We have a part to play, but the Holy Spirit is the One who causes the change to take place within us. You will not be the person in the future that you are today if you submit yourself to God's transformation process. You are going to be more like Jesus.

> Beloved, now we are children of God; and it has not yet been revealed what we shall be, but we know that when He is revealed, we shall be like Him, for we shall see Him as He is. And everyone who has this hope in Him purifies himself, just as He is pure.
>
> —1 John 3:2-3

What does it mean to purify oneself? Why is it necessary to have the Holy Spirit's power to accomplish this?

If we are all going to "be like Him," why do we need to purify ourselves now?

Transformed in Attitude

Christians are called upon to transform their minds from the way that the world thinks to the way that God thinks. Paul wrote in Romans 12:1–2:

> I beseech you therefore, brethren, by the mercies of God, that you present your bodies a living sacrifice, holy, acceptable to God, which is your reasonable service. And do not be conformed to this world, but be transformed by the renewing of your mind, that you may prove what is that good and acceptable and perfect will of God.

The two points of view—God's and man's—are nearly always opposite. The world tells you to get even with your enemies; God says to leave vengeance up to Him and to love your enemies, do good to them, and pray for them (Matthew 5:43–44, Romans 12:19–21). The world tells you to fight for your rights and defend yourself at all costs; God says to turn the other cheek (Matthew 5:38–39). The world tells you that hard work and education will result in success; God says that faith and obedience are what bring a person to success (Hebrews 11).

As Christians, we are called to think as God thinks, and then, with our renewed minds, to act as Jesus would act if He walked in our shoes on the earth today. A difference in thinking results in a difference in living.

> ...you should no longer walk as the rest of the Gentiles walk, in the futility of their mind, having their understanding darkened, being alienated from the life of God, because of the ignorance that is in them, because of the blindness of their heart; who, being past feeling, have given themselves over to lewdness, to work all uncleanness with greediness.

> —Ephesians 4:17-19

〜 Give some examples of the world's thinking that shows "the futility of their mind".

〜 How can you begin to renew your own mind to get rid of the attitudes that you listed above?

〜 God's Word Renews Our Thinking 〜

How can we renew our mind so that we think as Jesus thought? We acquire a renewed mind through a habit of reading God's Word regularly. Ephesians 5:26 refers to a cleansing by the "washing of water by the word." The more we read God's Word, the more the Word acts to cleanse our thoughts so that we think the pure thoughts of Christ. The more we read God's Word, the more we are confronted with God's truth. The Word of God convicts us of error and points out to us the need for change. It presents to us the truth and compels us to act on the truth.

The more we read God's Word, the more we become familiar with "God's opinion" and the more the Holy Spirit makes His opinion our opinion. The Word of God becomes *the way that we think*. And when that happens, we experience a genuine change. We begin to speak differently, act differently, make wiser choices, and adopt new priorities.

Our lives take on a new nature that flows from our new mind.

❧ How has your thinking changed since you became a Christian? How has reading the Word of God brought about change in your life?

> For the word of God is living and powerful, and sharper than any two-edged sword, piercing even to the division of soul and spirit, and of joints and marrow, and is a discerner of the thoughts and intents of the heart.
>
> —Hebrews 4:12

❧ When have you experienced the "living power" of God's Word in your own life? When has it been "sharper than any two-edged sword"?

∞ We Can Choose What We Think ∞

The mind is subject to the will. We have control over what we *choose* to think about. Paul wrote to the Corinthians that they should be engaged in "bringing every thought into captivity to the obedience of Christ" (2 Corinthians 10:5). We have the ability to screen, select, and cultivate what goes into our minds. We can keep our minds from wandering into evil thoughts by choosing to focus upon what is good in God's eyes (Philippians 4:8).

We also have the ability to choose *how* we will think. We have no control over some things that come into our field of vision or within our range of hearing as we live our daily lives, but we *do* have control over what we will think about, and how we will act on that information. For example, David *saw* Bathsheba. He wasn't looking for her. He was out walking on his balcony one night and he saw a beautiful woman bathing. That could have been the end of the story. David could have turned and walked back into his palace and thought nothing more about what he had seen.

Instead, David began to *think* about what he saw. He "sent and inquired about the woman." He did some research, he began to dwell in his mind on what it would be like to get a closer look at her and what it might be like to be with her. Eventually, he sent for her, sinned with her, and suffered serious consequences for that sin (2 Samuel 11:2–4).

When things come into our range of vision, we are to evaluate them with the "filter" of God's Word. If we find ourselves dwelling on a thought, we must ask ourselves, "Why am I thinking this? What is at the root of my thought? What will happen if I continue to think this way?" We do not need to act out of impulses, desires, and lusts. We can govern what we *choose* to think and then *choose* to do.

> Finally, brethren, whatever things are true, whatever things are noble, whatever things are just, whatever things are pure, whatever things are lovely, whatever things are of good report, if there is any virtue and if there is anything praiseworthy— meditate on these things.
>
> —Philippians 4:8

≪ Give practical examples of things that are: true; noble; just; pure; lovely; of good report.

≪ What does it mean to "meditate"? How is meditating on God's Word different from the "meditation" practiced in Eastern religions, such as yoga?

∞ God's Truth Planted in Our Memories ∞

What we put into our minds is what we have in our "memory bank." One of the ways that the Holy Spirit helps us is by bringing to mind what Jesus said (John 14:26). When we commit the Word of God to memory or even read God's Word repeatedly as a life habit, the Holy Spirit can then bring God's Word quickly to our minds when we are making a decision or facing a problem. His "answer" becomes the thought that drives our actions. In this way, the Holy Spirit effects change within us. No longer are we limited only to our own intellect, emotions, and memories of what we have learned and experienced—our lives have a new foundation of God's Word on which to make right choices.

Many people are discouraged today because they are confused, plagued by recurring negative thoughts, or because they don't know which way to turn in their lives. What an encouraging word you can share with them that God can transform their lives by the renewing of their minds! They can experience a real change in their lives, one that begins in the way they think.

> But the Helper, the Holy Spirit, whom the Father will send in My name, He will teach you all things, and bring to your remembrance all things that I said to you.
>
> —John 14:26

How does "remembering" things affect the way that you think? What does this process have to do with "renewing your mind"?

Conformed to Christ's Image

Being *transformed* begins in the mind, and being *conformed* begins with our habits. God's desire is that we become more and more like Jesus in the things that we do, which means that our "automatic responses" to life—our habitual daily rituals and the routine way in which we handle life—must reflect Christ's nature.

Paul wrote in Romans 8:29 that God wants us to "be conformed to the image of His Son." We all know the phrase "Like father, like son." In our case, we are to be "like Father, like Son."

94

∞ Christ in Us ∞

The process of being conformed begins with Christ dwelling within us. His Spirit occupies and fills our spirit. Jesus told His disciples that the Holy Spirit would dwell within them (John 14:17). Paul wrote repeatedly that the "Spirit of God dwells in you," that we have "the Spirit of Christ," and that "Christ is in you" (Romans 8:9–10).

Christ is not just "added" to our life; His very nature is implanted within us. If anything, the process becomes one of subtraction—He removes from us all the old habits and automatic behaviors that are not like Christ. God chisels away at us, chipping off the old dead patterns of behavior. He often uses painful methods to bring us to the realization that we are *not* acting as Christ would act. Sometimes He uses family members, friends, failures, financial setbacks, or even physical ailments to cause us to face our lives and ask, "What is God trying to strip away from me so that I am more like Jesus?"

∞ What has God done in your life to "chip away" old patterns of behavior? How has He made your own life more like Christ?

But if we walk in the light as He is in the light, we have fellowship with one another, and the blood of Jesus Christ His Son cleanses us from all sin. If we say that we have no sin, we deceive ourselves, and the truth is not in us.

—1 John 1:7-8

95

☙ What does it mean to "walk in the light"? Give practical examples.

☙ How does "fellowship with one another" help the Holy Spirit's work of conforming us to Christ's image?

∞ Abiding in Christ ∞

God works to conform us to Christ in order to bring us to a greater trust and reliance upon Him, submitting our will to His. The picture that Jesus used to depict this conformation process was one of a vine and its branches. Jesus said in John 15:4–5, 7–8:

> Abide in Me, and I in you. As the branch cannot bear fruit of itself, unless it abides in the vine, neither can you, unless you abide in Me. I am the vine, you are the branches. He who abides in Me, and I in him, bears much fruit; for without Me you can do nothing...If you abide in Me, and My words abide in you, you will ask what you desire, and it shall be done for you. By this My Father is glorified, that you bear much fruit; so you will be My disciples.

When you look at a vine, it is virtually impossible to tell where the vine ends and the branches begin. The sap flows through a vine into its branches, pushing out growth and producing fruit. It is a *living* process, not a mechanical one.

Jesus calls each of us to abide in Him—to rely solely upon His Holy Spirit to give life to our spirits. Ultimately, as we live in Christ and He lives in us, the Holy Spirit conforms us fully to Christ's nature. Sinning becomes foreign to us; righteousness becomes the norm of our lives (1 John 3:5–6, 5:18).

What exactly is it that is conformed? Our speech and our behaviors. We speak what is true, loving, and right. We do what is righteous, loving, and of most help. We respond to life's circumstances and situations just as Jesus would respond to them.

In a practical way, how do we "abide" in Christ? Jesus said, "If My words abide in you." Again, we must take the Word of God into our lives so that we fully understand God's commandments and the way that God wants us to live. This goes beyond a frequent reading of God's Word to a real study of God's Word. God's Word abides in us when we seek out the deeper riches of meaning in it. Study takes time and requires focus, but it is something that is possible for every person.

We also abide in Christ by communicating with God on a continual basis. Prayer becomes a way of life for us. We are always consulting God in our spirits. We are always mindful of His presence. We are always in a state of thanksgiving and praise and appreciation for what He is doing for us, in us, and through us. We talk to God regularly—in our minds and in our spoken words of praise and petition.

We spend time alone with God, listening for Him to speak to us. We share with Him the innermost secrets and desires of our hearts. We develop a *spiritually intimate* relationship with God. And the encouraging news is that every Christian believer can do this! Each of us can choose to spend time in the Word, in prayer, and in listening to God.

> And this I pray, that your love may abound still more and more in knowledge and all discernment, that you may approve the things that are excellent, that you may be sincere and without offense till the day of Christ, being filled with the fruits of righteousness which are by Jesus Christ, to the glory and praise of God.
>
> —Philippians 1:9-11

What does Paul mean when he speaks of love that abounds in "knowledge" and "discernment"? Why are these qualities important in understanding love?

How does a person gain "knowledge" and "discernment"? How do these qualities help us to "approve the things that are excellent"?

Be diligent to present yourself approved to God, a worker who does not need to be ashamed, rightly dividing the word of truth. But shun profane and idle babblings, for they will increase to more ungodliness. And their message will spread like cancer.

—2 Timothy 2:15-17

❧ What does it mean to be "rightly dividing the word of truth"? How does a person learn to do this?

❧ Give practical examples of "profane and idle babblings". How does such talk "increase to more ungodliness"? Give examples of Christ-like conversation.

--- ❧ **Today and Tomorrow** ❧ ---

TODAY: MY TRANSFORMATION STARTS IN MY MIND, AND CARRIES OUT IN MY DAILY HABITS.

TOMORROW: I WILL SPEND TIME EACH DAY THIS COMING WEEK MEDITATING ON GOD'S WORD.

God Has a Way Through the Storm

ꙮ In This Lesson ꙮ

LEARNING: WHAT CAUSES LIFE'S STORMY TIMES?

GROWING: HOW AM I SUPPOSED TO RESPOND TO SUFFERING AND TRIALS?

ꙮ

At no time in the teachings of Jesus do we find a promise that we are exempt from the struggles, suffering, and storms of life. Rather, what we find is that:

ꙮ God will be with us in the storms

ꙮ God is greater than any storm

ꙮ God will bring us through life's storms as we trust in Him

ꙮ God will always use a storm for our ultimate good—to strengthen us, refine us, and bring us good

At no time, however, are we promised a storm-free life. Our challenge is not to spend our efforts trying to avoid the inevitable but to prepare our spirits for stormy times. Peter wrote this to the early church as it faced Roman persecution (1 Peter 1:13):

Gird up the loins of your mind, be sober, and rest your hope fully upon the grace that is to be brought to you at the revelation of Jesus Christ.

Peter's advice is not, "Here's how to escape the storm." Rather, he tells these believers who were facing intense times of trial, "Here's how to *prepare* for the trouble ahead."

The Nature of Storms

Generally speaking, there are two types of storms: ones that strike us suddenly and without warning, and storms that we see coming, often long in advance. Both types of storms come our way. There is no escaping them. Storms generally have three origins.

1. *There are storms that we create.* We often hate to admit this fact, but we cause many of the problems that we face in life—sometimes willfully and out of a rebellious spirit, but often innocently and out of ignorance.

2. *There are storms that are created by others.* Far fewer storms are created by others than most people claim. We are all prone to self-justification and blaming others for our problems. Still, there are some storms that legitimately are caused by other people.

3. *There are storms that are created by general circumstances.* Natural disasters, general mechanical equipment, and depletion of resources are examples. A flood would be a "storm" that might be considered circumstantial.

🐚 When have you experienced storms in your life from any of these three areas: Self-induced storm; Storm caused by others; Circumstantial storm?

What God Says about Storms

The Word of God gives us seven important truths about the storms that blow into our lives:

1. Storms come to all people, Christians and non-Christians.

2. Jesus knows all about the storm in your life.

3. God doesn't always deal with the storm in the way that we think He should.

4. Jesus always offers a word of comfort in the storm.

5. Jesus always issues a command in the midst of the storm.

6. Jesus gives us power to obey His storm-related command.

7. We always come face-to-face with important truths as the result of storms.

Many of these truths can be seen in the story of Jesus and his disciples during a stormy night in Galilee.

Read Matthew 14:22–33.

How we respond to storms is more important than determining what caused a storm. We are not called by God to understand *why* storms come our way as much as we are called by God to *respond* to storms in a godly way, causing us to grow in our trust of God and to witness to others of God's presence in our lives.

Knowing the origin of a storm may be an important clue as to what God desires to teach us from a storm, but it is never the sole lesson that God has for us. We discover the greater lesson by looking at what we *do* when storms strike us.

> But when he saw that the wind was boisterous, he was afraid; and beginning to sink he cried out, saying, "Lord, save me!" And immediately Jesus stretched out His hand and caught him, and said to him, "O you of little faith, why did you doubt?"
>
> —Matthew 14:30-31

❧ What probably caused Peter's fear in this situation? What caused his *doubt*? How are the two different?

❧ What was Peter's response? What would *you* have done?

103

∞ Storms Come to All People ∞

Storms come into the lives of the righteous as well as the unrighteous. Jesus had fed 5,000 men and their families during the day that preceded this stormy night. Then He had commanded His disciples to cross the sea while He went aside to spend time alone with His Heavenly Father. The disciples had done nothing wrong. They were not being corrected by God for an error or sin.

You may not have done anything wrong either to cause the storm that comes into your life. Some storms are sent by God for purposes other than correction. These are storms that God *allows* to come our way, as opposed to deliberately *sending* them. He will use such storms to bring about our perfection.

> My brethren, count it all joy when you fall into various trials, knowing that the testing of your faith produces patience. But let patience have its perfect work, that you may be perfect and complete, lacking nothing.
>
> —James 1:2-4

∞ When have you "counted it all joy" when you found yourself in a trial? What is your usual response?

∞ What does it mean to "let patience have its perfect work"? How do we accomplish this?

∽ Jesus Knows About the Storm ∽

Jesus knew that His disciples were in a storm, and He knows when you are in a storm. The Sea of Galilee is not a large sea. Under normal conditions, a group of men can row a boat across it in a matter of two hours. So wherever Jesus was praying, the storm was also blowing there! Jesus also knew that this natural storm caused an "inner storm" in the lives of His disciples. He had seen them before during a stormy time, and He knew their hearts.

> Are not five sparrows sold for two copper coins? And not one of them is forgotten before God. But the very hairs of your head are all numbered. Do not fear therefore; you are of more value than many sparrows.

> —Luke 12:6-7

∽ Why does Jesus emphasize how inexpensive sparrows were? What did this suggest about God's concern for birds?

∽ What does this suggest for God's concern about you? Why does Jesus say that He knows how many hairs are on your head? Do *you* know that number?

∽ God's Methods Are Higher ∽

The Bible tells us that Jesus sent His disciples away in a boat and was alone with the Father "when evening came." He did not come to them on the stormy sea until the "fourth watch," which is the time from 3 AM to 6 AM. The disciples might have preferred that Jesus come to them the instant the storm struck them. They certainly would have preferred for Him to arrive before they were completely worn out from eight or more hours of rowing! Jesus, however, came to them at precisely the moment when He knew that His purposes would be accomplished.

Indeed, we have no mention in this story that the disciples cried out to Jesus prior to His arrival or that they had used their faith in any way during their struggle against the storm's winds and waves. We need to cry sooner, as opposed to later, when storms strike. Furthermore, Jesus came in a way that was totally unexpected. He appeared to them walking on water, something that the disciples had never seen before.

"For My thoughts are not your thoughts, Nor are your ways My ways," says the LORD. "For as the heavens are higher than the earth, So are My ways higher than your ways, And My thoughts than your thoughts."

—Isaiah 55:8-9

∽ When have you seen God act in your own life in surprising ways? How were His ways different from what you might have expected?

∝ When have you waited until the last possible moment to call out for God's help? How might things have been different if you had called out sooner?

∝ A Word of Comfort ∝

Jesus always gives a word of encouragement and comfort to us. Regardless of the intensity of the storm or how ominous the trouble, Jesus' word to us is always a word of encouragement—not an idle word of optimism, but a word of power and strength. The encouraging word that Jesus speaks to us in the secret place of our heart is a sure reality—it does come to pass!

As the disciples struggled in their storm, the word of Jesus to them was this: "Be of good cheer! It is I; do not be afraid" (Matthew 14:27). Jesus speaks the same message to us: "Be glad. I'm here. Don't be afraid." Regardless of what Jesus may say to you about your storm, He will *always* assure you of His presence with you.

> These things I have spoken to you, that in Me you may have peace. In the world you will have tribulation; but be of good cheer, I have overcome the world.
>
> —John 16:33

∝ If Jesus has "overcome the world", why do we still face tribulation? What is His purpose in allowing trials in our lives?

✎ How can this knowledge bring encouragement to you during times of trouble? Who else might be needing this word of encouragement this week?

∞ Jesus Gives a Command ∞

Jesus always gives a command in the midst of the storm. He gives direction in every stormy situation that we find in the New Testament. His command is either to the storm or to us. On one occasion, Jesus spoke directly to a storm, saying, "Peace, be still!" (Mark 4:39). When Jesus walked to His disciples on a stormy sea, He gave a command to Peter: "Come!"

In your time of tribulation, you can always be assured that Jesus is either going to rebuke the trouble (including dealing with a troublemaker), or He is going to call you to do something in the midst of the trouble that will strengthen, purify, or otherwise change you. Look for His command.

During stormy times, we must do the following:

✎ *Turn to God,* putting our eyes on Him, not on the storm.

✎ *Ask God, "What do You want me to do?* Ask, "Am I to use my faith against this storm? Am I to grow in trust by riding out this storm?"

✎ *Do what God tells you to do.* The acid test of faith is always obedience. It is not enough to hear God's command in the storm. We must obey His command.

I will instruct you and teach you in the way you should go; I will guide you with My eye.

—Psalm 32:8

❧ When have you been guided to take action during a time of tribulation? How did God's direction bring you peace?

❧ What does the Psalmist mean the God will "guide you with My eye"? Why His eye? What does this suggest about God's awareness of your sufferings?

∞ Power to Obey ∞

The Holy Spirit empowers and equips us to carry out God's commands. He gives us the courage, the strength, and the ability that we need to act in obedience. Jesus said to Peter, "Come!"—and then He gave him the ability to walk on water. Peter did not have that ability in himself. He had never walked on water before, and we have no evidence that he walked on water after that night. Peter was enabled to walk on water in direct response to Jesus' command.

Do not hesitate to obey what God tells you to do in the midst of your trouble or trial. He will enable you to carry out His command. If He tells you to endure in patience, He will give you the strength to endure in patience. If He tells you to speak to your storm with faith, He will make your faith effective in calming the storm. Whatever God *commands* you to do, He will *equip* you to do. Your part is to obey.

> But this is what I commanded them, saying, "Obey My voice, and I will be your God, and you shall be My people. And walk in all the ways that I have commanded you, that it may be well with you."

> —Jeremiah 7:23

~ Are there any commands of God that you are not obeying at present? How might this be adding unnecessary suffering in your life?

∞ Discovery in Storms ∞

It is in storms that we often discover the most important truths of our lives. I can guarantee that Peter never forgot the night that he walked on water. He also never forgot what he learned from Jesus that night:

~ Jesus was preparing him for his future.

~ Jesus was revealing His absolute power over all things.

❧ Jesus was building up his faith.

❧ Jesus was bringing him to the point where he would say, "Truly You are the Son of God."

I do not know all of the lessons that God may teach you as you experience storms, trials, tribulations, and difficulties in your life. I do not know the precise lessons that you will encounter in pain, suffering, and trouble. I do know this: God will always reveal to you something about Himself that will build you up in your inner person and prepare you for greater days ahead.

His lesson to you will be uniquely *for you*. The lesson that someone else experiences out of the same storm may not be the lesson that God is giving to you. Look for what He is speaking to your heart and what He is doing in your life. Most importantly, don't miss out on the lesson that God has for you in the storm. Don't just ride out the storm and then forget what has happened to you. God has a purpose in every storm, and one of those purposes is to change some aspect of your life so that you become more like Jesus.

> The LORD looks from heaven; He sees all the sons of men.... He fashions their hearts individually; He considers all their works.
>
> —Psalm 33:13, 15

❧ How does it bring you encouragement to know that God "fashions men's hearts individually"?

 If God pays attention to all your works, in what way might trials sometimes reflect our own deeds?

Our Response to Storms

God's desire is that we turn to Him during a time of trouble and keep our eyes focused squarely on Him. We are to continue to praise Him and to thank Him for His faithfulness to us. In all things, we are to give God praise and honor and glory.

Many people who are hit with trouble respond in one of these ways:

 Ignore God: They turn all of their attention to the trial or storm and never think to consult God.

 Blame God: They never consider the full purposes of God in the storm or even the origin of the storm.

 Rebel against God: They say to themselves, "Why serve God if this is what happens?"

The Christian is called to do just the opposite: We are to turn to God the instant that trouble hits, ask God to reveal all that He desires to reveal about the origin and response that we are to have against the storm, and trust God to bring about His good purposes in our lives, both during and as the result of the storm. Praise God regardless. He is at work in storms and in fair-weather times!

Take a few minutes to reflect upon a storm that you are currently experiencing or one that another person is experiencing. Then respond to these questions:

❧ In what ways is God encouraging you by these passages from His Word?

❧ Who might He be leading you to share this encouragement with?

...but we also glory in tribulations, knowing that tribulation produces perseverance; and perseverance, character; and character, hope.

—Romans 5:3-4

∝ How does perseverance lead to character? How does character lead to hope?

∝ When have you seen trials in your own life lead to perseverance? What character and hope has this led to?

∝ Today and Tomorrow ∝

TODAY: THE WAY THAT I RESPOND TO A STORM IS MORE IMPORTANT THAN FIGURING OUT WHAT CAUSED THE STORM.

TOMORROW: I WILL CONSCIOUSLY THANK GOD THIS WEEK FOR THE STORMS THAT HE ALLOWS IN MY LIFE.

LESSON 10

God Will Give You His Answer

LEARNING: WHO AM I IN GOD'S EYES?

GROWING: WHAT IS GOD'S PURPOSE FOR MY LIFE?

We must never be ashamed of having questions or honest doubts. Our questions are the starting point of our search for truth, meaning, and fulfillment in life. The two general questions that every mature person asks at some point are well known:

🙠 *Who am I?*

🙠 *Why am I here?*

These questions are what I call *identity* questions. They are at the very core of our humanity. We want to know our nature and the purpose for our creation. But three other questions relate to specific circumstances or problems. I call them *situational* questions:

🙠 *What is going on?*

🙠 *Why is this happening?*

🙠 *What should I do?*

The encouraging news is that God has answers to each of these questions, and He delights in sharing them with us.

Identity Questions

When we ask the questions "Who am I?" and "Why am I here?" we are really asking two other questions: "Who is God?" and "What is God doing?" Our two identity questions are answered when we answer these questions about God's identity.

The Bible tells us that God is Creator. "In the beginning, God created" (Genesis 1:1). He created the heavens and the earth and all that is in them—including us. He is our Maker, our Source, our Author. Who are you? You are a creation of God, uniquely gifted and designed by Him for a specific role and function on this earth.

Consider these words: Creator, Maker, Source, Author. Creator of what? Maker of what? Source of what? Author of what? These very words imply that God has a plan and a purpose for this world and for each person whom He creates.

A creator creates a place and creatures to occupy it. A maker makes things happen; he sets in motion functions and processes. A source provides all that is necessary for a purpose to be accomplished. An author writes a message that conveys meaning and instructions, as well as words of inspiration or commands.

If you truly desire to know who you are and why you are here, the Bible gives you the answers. You are one of God's creations, unique in all ways and fashioned very specifically for a purpose that God has in mind. You are put into this world to make something happen—you have been created for a specific function in God's plan. The Holy Spirit has been given to you to help you carry out your function. All around you, God is engineering the situations and circumstances necessary for you to fulfill your function as you obey Him.

On a daily basis, God is giving to you all that you need to carry out His plan for you. God has given you your unique set of talents and traits, and He is providing your energy, time, and abundant resources to carry out your function.

You are a "living letter" being written by God to communicate God's love and forgiveness to those around you. You are a living testimony to the redemption work of Jesus Christ. When you choose to obey God's call upon your life, you become a living example of God's Word in the world today.

 How has God revealed to you your role in His plan for all mankind?

 What is it that you do well when you use the gifts that He has given to you?

 How has God challenged you to live in obedience to Him, and to express His love and forgiveness to others?

∞ Situational Questions ∞

When we ask, "What is going on? Why is this happening? What should I do?" we must always ask in relationship to God's plan and purposes for us:

🙐 What is **God** doing?

🙐 What does **God** intend to happen through this situation?

🙐 How does **God** want me to respond?

Again, our answers to these questions are to be found in God's Word. As we read God's Word, we can trust the Holy Spirit to reveal God's answers so that we know with certainty what God wants us to know and to respond as God wants us to respond. The Bible tells us that God wants us to have His wisdom. James 1:5–6 assures us:

> If any of you lacks wisdom, let him ask of God, who gives to all liberally and without reproach, and it will be given to him. But let him ask in faith, with no doubting, for he who doubts is like a wave of the sea driven and tossed by the wind.

James tells us three important things about finding God's answers:

1. **We are to ask in faith.** We must believe that, when we ask for wisdom from God, He will give it to us. We must accept the answer that we have heard from God and act on it. If we second-guess what we believe God is saying to us, James says that we are going to be "tossed" about and we will be unstable in our actions (James 1:6–8).

As you go to God for answers, *expect* Him to give you answers. Have an open heart ready to receive His answers as you study the Scriptures and listen to the Holy Spirit in your heart.

2. ***God will give us wisdom liberally.*** In other words, He will give us the fullness of the answer that we need to have. He will not keep a secret from us when we need His wisdom. This does not mean that God will tell us everything that we *want* to know. It means that God will tell us everything that we *need* to know from His perspective. Some things will always remain a mystery to us because there simply is no way that we, as finite creatures, can ever comprehend the fullness of God's majesty—His omnipotence, His omniscience, His glory. There are many things that we cannot understand about God's nature. They are too awesome for our minds and hearts to contain.

The broader message, however, is this: God always tells us what we *need* to know in order to live out His commandments, be a witness to Christ Jesus, and fulfill His specific role and function for our lives. He keeps no secrets regarding His statutes, the nature of Christ, or the purpose that He has for us to be agents of God's love and forgiveness. He always tells us what we need to know to do the work that He has created for us to do. Trust God to give you such information *liberally*.

3. ***God does not criticize us for asking.*** God gives us His wisdom "without reproach." He does not chide us for doubting. He does not ridicule us for not knowing already. God never considers any question too small or any problem insignificant. He is the God of eternal truth, and He is the God of factual details. You should feel free to ask God *any* question about your life, your current circumstances, and the next steps that God wants you to take.

When have you faced a situation where you realized that you lacked wisdom? What did you do?

∽ When have you asked God for wisdom and received new insight? When have you struggled with a lack of faith?

∽ Searching the Scriptures for Specific Answers ∽

When you are faced with a situation that baffles you, spend some concentrated time in God's Word. Use a concordance and identify several key concepts that you believe are related to your question. Then read the Scriptures that are listed under that topic. Make notes to yourself about the meaning that you see in each verse. Before you begin reading the Scriptures, invite the Holy Spirit to speak to your heart as you read. Open yourself to hearing His voice in your innermost being. He usually speaks to us through strong impressions, sudden new ideas or insights, and through ideas and concepts that we just can't seem to shake after we have finished our study time.

In the course of your reading on a particular topic, other concepts may come to mind, or you may have questions about specific words or phrases that you encounter. Spend some time searching the Scriptures on those topics. The Holy Spirit may also remind you of a passage of Scripture that you have read or studied at a previous time. Follow His lead in your study.

Give yourself several hours—perhaps even several days or weeks—to search the Scriptures before you come to a conclusion about God's answer to you. Now, in some cases, you may find your answer in the first verse that you study. More likely, though, the truth is to be found as you read and study "precept upon precept, Line upon line, Here a little, there a little" (Isaiah 28:10).

Keep in mind always that God will never give you a directive that is not confirmed in His Word. He will not tell you to do something that is contrary to His commandments, to the life of Jesus Christ, or to the teachings of the Bible as a whole. He will not tell you to do something that will bring spiritual harm to another person or that will be a stumbling block to others. John wrote: "He who loves his brother abides in the light, and there is no cause for stumbling in him" (1 John 2:10).

When God reveals His specific answer to your specific question, you then have a responsibility to act upon that answer.

> But be doers of the word, and not hearers only, deceiving yourselves. For if anyone is a hearer of the word and not a doer, he is like a man observing his natural face in a mirror; for he observes himself, goes away, and immediately forgets what kind of man he was. But he who looks into the perfect law of liberty and continues in it, and is not a forgetful hearer but a doer of the work, this one will be blessed in what he does.
>
> —James 1:22-25

How do we deceive ourselves when we hear God's word without putting it into practice? What result does this have in our lives?

Give practical examples of how looking in the mirror is beneficial. What does this tell us about God's Word?

Answers Are Encouraging

When God answers our questions about our identity, and when He provides direction for us to take in puzzling situations, we cannot help but feel encouraged! We have been given a purpose in life. We have a job that we are equipped to do and can succeed at doing as we trust the Holy Spirit. Our lives can be filled with meaning, and we can know the satisfaction that comes with serving God effectively.

You can encourage others by telling them these two truths:

> God has a purpose for your life. He has gifted you in special ways to do a specific job.

> God has an answer to your questions. He wants you to live in His wisdom, day by day.

You may not have answers to the questions that people ask you, but you can always say, "I don't know. But I know the One who does! Let's ask God." Be quick to pray with others that they might turn to God for the answers that they need to the big questions about their lives, and to the immediate questions that they have about their circumstances. Be quick to point others toward the riches of God's Word—it is the Answer Book to life's most puzzling test questions.

So God created man in His own image; in the image of God He created him; male and female He created them.

—Genesis 1:27

꙾ How does understanding who God is help you to understand who you are?

꙾ What aspects of who you are reflect the image of God?

> Looking unto Jesus, the author and finisher of our faith, who for the joy that was set before Him endured the cross, despising the shame, and has sat down at the right hand of the throne of God.
>
> —Hebrews 12:2

꙾ What is the difference between being an "author" and a "finisher"?

꙾ What areas of your life are still unfinished? How does this verse encourage you, in spite of your own shortcomings?

All Scripture is given by inspiration of God, and is profitable for doctrine, for reproof, for correction, for instruction in righteousness.

—2 Timothy 3:16

❧ Define each of these things: doctrine; reproof; correction; instruction. How does each differ?

❧ What does this verse suggest about how we can gain wisdom and insight into God's will?

❧ Today and Tomorrow ❧

Today: God is eager to give me more wisdom, that I may understand Him more fully.

Tomorrow: I will spend time this week in a deep study of His Word, on a topic that is pertinent to my life.